# 50 PRINCIPLES TO THRIVE IN LIFE

## From Half-Full to Overflowing

© Copyright Action Takers Publishing Inc 2024

All rights reserved. No part of this publication may be reproduced or transmitted in any form or by any means, mechanical or electronic, including photocopying and recording, or by any information storage and retrieval system, without permission in writing from publisher (except by reviewer, who may quote brief sections and/or show brief video clips in a review).

**Disclaimer:** The Publisher and Author make no representations or warranties with respect to the accuracy or completeness of the contents of this work and specifically disclaims all warranties, including without limitation warranties of fitness for a particular purpose. No warranty may be created or suitable for every situation. This works is sold with the understanding that neither the Publisher nor the Author are not engaged in rendering legal, accounting, or other professional services. If professional assistance is required, the services of a competent professional person should be sought.

Neither the Publisher nor the Author shall be liable for damages arising herefrom. The fact that an organization or website is referred to in this work as a referred source of further information does not mean that the Author or the Publisher endorse the information the organization or website may provide or recommendations it may make. Further, readers should be aware that websites listed in this work may have changed or disappeared between when this work was written and when it was read.

ISBN # (paperback) 978-1-956665-71-0
ISBN # (Kindle) 978-1-956665-72-7

Email: lynda@actiontakerspublishing.com
Website: www.actiontakerspublishing.com
Published by Action Takers Publishing™

Ghostwritten by Laura Huber
Cover design by Salman Sarwar

# Table of Contents

Acknowledgments ................................................................... vii

Introduction ............................................................................. 1

Principle #1: Embrace Your Foundation ................................... 3

Principle #2: Take Pride in Your Name .................................... 7

Principle #3: Ice Cube, Carrot, Egg, or Coffee Bean ............... 11

Principle #4: Lean Into Your Insecurities ............................... 15

Principle #5: Structure Your Day ............................................ 19

Principle #6: Control the Controllables .................................. 25

Principle #7: Preparation Creates Swagger ............................ 29

Principle #8: Trust the Process ............................................... 31

Principle #9: Find a Hobby ..................................................... 35

Principle #10: Create a Fun Workout Routine ....................... 39

Principle #11: Remain Curious ............................................... 43

Principle #12: Tons of Accountability and a Dose of Grace .... 47

Principle #13: Forgiveness ...................................................... 53

Principle #14: Give a Little to Get a Little .............................. 57

Principle #15: Love the Journey ............................................. 61

Principle #16: Companionship ................................................ 65

Principle #17: Sacrifices Must Be Made .................................. 69

Principle #18: Be Comfortable Being Uncomfortable ............ 73

# TABLE OF CONTENTS

Principle #19: Toe the Line Between Confidence and Cocky ............... 77

Principle #20: Get Your Seven Laughs ................... 81

Principle #21: Meditate ................... 85

Principle #22: There's Only One You, Be You ................... 91

Principle #23: Flowers for the Living ................... 95

Principle #24: Manage Your Expectations ................... 101

Principle #25: Mentorship is Crucial ................... 107

Principle #26: Embrace Criticism ................... 113

Principle #27: Identify the Fruit on the Tree ................... 117

Principle #28: Always Look to Add Value ................... 121

Principle #29: Love Boldly ................... 125

Principle #30: Have Lunch with the Loner ................... 129

Principle #31: Stand for Something or Fall for Anything ................... 133

Principle #32: Identify Your Why(s) ................... 137

Principle #33: Read Books That Are Foreign to Your Life ................... 143

Principle #34: Therapy, Therapy, Therapy ................... 147

Principle #35: Representation Matters ................... 153

Principle #36: Respect the Clock ................... 157

Principle #37: Proverbs 27:17 ................... 161

Principle #38: Unlearn to Relearn ................... 165

Principle #39: Spiritual Foundation ................... 169

Principle #40: Borrow Some Sense ................... 173

Principle #41: Philanthropy ................... 177

Principle #42: Patience Before Progress ................................................. 181

Principle #43: Belief and Faith; a Beautiful Duo ................................. 185

Principle #44: It's a Marathon, Not a Sprint ........................................ 189

Principle #45: Celebrate Every Victory ................................................. 195

Principle #46: The Power of Words and Energy ................................ 199

Principle #47: Toe the Line with Delusion .......................................... 205

Principle #48: Leave the Gavel to the Judge ....................................... 209

Principle #49: Control Your Movement: Don't Confuse Movement with Progress ................................................................. 213

Principle #50: The 50% Rule ................................................................... 217

Conclusion ................................................................................................... 221

# Acknowledgments

I'd be remiss to not begin such an important venture without gratitude. I'd first like to thank God, for all of His creations. They've all collectively indirectly or directly culminated my life experiences. I owe all my praises to Him.

Secondly, I'd like to thank my wonderful mother, Diane Smith. The examples she's unknowingly given me by how she lives her life are irreplaceable. Her conscious guidance and tutelage gave me a strong foundation to thrive on this planet.

There's a host of family members that would take several pages to name each individually, but in short, they're all loved and held near to my heart. Likewise, those that I consider friends are vital to my progression and success. To all that fall into these categories: thank you.

There's a group of people that I consider mentors, whom I can't wait for them all to read about in this book and learn just how instrumental they have been on my journey. To all of them, I'm forever grateful.

To my ancestors; Mr. Thomas Jefferson Moore, my Great-Great grandfather, his daughter (my great grandmother) Ms. Ezella "Mama E" Moffett, your spirits guide me. Your strength and gumption give me the confidence that I can conquer all. To the known and unknown ancestors that guide and protect me from things unseen, I am gracious. I aim to make you all proud.

To my first manager, Gail Tassell, I'm grateful for you taking a chance on a young man from Opelika, AL who had nothing to offer but gratitude, unrefined talent, and a dream.

## ACKNOWLEDGMENTS

To the reader, yes you, thank you. Thank you for giving this book a shot. Your interest in my perspective is indeed enough for me to drop tears as I write this. My wish is that you take away a few things that add undeniable value to your life.

# Introduction

What is the meaning of life?

When I'm asked this question, I go to the most basic way of looking at it. To give back to our Creator and to help one another. I think that's why we're here.

I found this truth very early on. Once I identified that—it resonated with me. I realized that I was my full true self whenever I was giving to others, especially young people.

I was giving back even when I was a very young adult in college. I volunteered so much that two years in a row I won the national award for the *Collegiate Athlete with the Most Community Service Hours*. Frankly, half of my free time was spent with the children in group homes. I helped them with their homework, played video and board games with them, read to them, and sometimes took them to restaurants to get a taste of the good ol' fast food world. I just felt like it was part of my calling.

I'm still finding ways to give back. I love speaking to students around the country about my journey and general life advice. I truly appreciate and enjoy when their parents are present because I believe parents play such an important role in shaping their children's dreams. Children naturally look up to their parents, valuing their opinions deeply, and often put a lot of weight on what their parents think they can or cannot achieve. That's why I emphasize to parents how important it is to nurture and support their child's dreams, whatever they may be. I warn them to be careful because sometimes parents can unintentionally discourage their children's dreams under the cloak of love and protection. That lesson resonates deeply with me because I know what it's like to have a dream that feels out of reach.

Growing up in Opelika, Alabama, my own journey began with a dream I discovered as early as six years old: I wanted to be an actor. I

## INTRODUCTION

lived half the time on my grandmother's farm and half the time with my mom in the city of Opelika. I already knew at the age of six that I wanted to be an actor, but the only actor I'd ever seen was on TV. In Opelika, there weren't any actors to be found unless I turned on the television.

But I was brave and had so much gumption that I was able to go for my dream of becoming an actor and actually accomplishing it. By doing so, it naturally brought many people to me asking for advice. I wanted to help everyone who came to me, so I thought I better think of a way to help the millions of people who want to know how I did it.

I decided that writing down 50 principles of what got me to where I am today seemed like the right thing to do. These 50 principles brought me to this point and keep carrying me further and further. It is my hope that, like me, you will be uplifted and encouraged by each and every one of them. I pray that they give you the strength and wisdom that you need when confronted with any challenges that life may throw your way.

As you read through these principles, I want you to think about how each one can transform your perspective, enhance your relationships, and empower you to thrive in all areas of your life. Reflect on the challenges you've faced, the lessons you've learned, and the goals you still want to achieve as you embrace the journey of becoming the best version of yourself.

As you read through these principles, I want you to think about how they apply to your own life—your experiences, your challenges, and your aspirations. Consider where you are now, where you want to be, and what changes you can make to align your actions with your values. Let these principles inspire you to take meaningful steps toward the life you truly want to create.

# PRINCIPLE #1

## Embrace Your Foundation

*"We are our history. That is the only way that we can be present."* —Ralph Ellison

Growing up in Opelika, Alabama, was a unique experience for me, that was different from many of my peers. Though the name Opelika comes from the Native Muskogean language meaning "big swamp," you won't find any swamps to explore there. So, I found my own kind of adventure in the everyday responsibilities and experiences that shaped my life.

For most of my childhood my mom, Cynthia Diane Smith, was a single mother raising me and my older brother, Tyrone Terrell McKissic, on her own. I had a stepfather, Robert DuBose, for about five years of my childhood. We still have a good relationship today, but after their divorce it was just my mom raising us. She worked a lot, so most of our days off from school were spent in Salem, Alabama at my grandmother's. My brother and I would start the summer in Opelika, but after enough evenings of worrying our mother, off to Salem we went.

Looking back, I'm sure my mother knew that this was a good place for her sons to learn about life, love, and having a legacy.

Going to grandmother's house was like stepping back in time. The house was built by my great, great grandfather, Thomas Jefferson Moore, way back in 1910, so it was missing many modern conveniences. For a city boy it wasn't easy—it was a total mindset shift. One of the things grandmother's old house was missing was central air—and Alabama summers are blazing hot! So, grandmother had a few metal fans to stir the hot air around. Another convenience my grandmother's house was missing was indoor plumbing. That meant if I woke up in the middle of the night and needed to use the restroom, I would hold it until morning, because I was too scared to go out into the dark night for a stroll down to the outhouse. Here I was, a young boy in 1990 using an outhouse.

Grandmother's house might have been missing many things, but one thing it had for sure was structure. There was a strict routine we had to live by, and it started with the roosters crowing. That meant the sun was rising and it was time to wake up.

The first thing every morning, my great-grandmother, who lived with my grandmother, would get up, open the door, and call the cows. Then the two grandmas would come in and get us up. Our first job was to boil water. We had well water coming into the house, but it wasn't hot. So, we would boil the water, wash our faces, brush our teeth, and then head outside to feed the cows and the chickens. Before coming back in, we gathered all the eggs and great-grandmother would cook us fresh eggs for breakfast.

There was structure there that we couldn't budge on. The animals always had to be fed, the chickens' eggs always had to be gathered, and many other little things that had to get done before the day was over.

Having cows on the farm meant there was going to be a lot of hard work. Including fixing fences and making hay. Lifting 50-pound bales of hay in the hot Alabama sun is a good way to get in shape and build some muscle. Even though I wasn't thinking about that kind of stuff back then, I understood something even more important very early in life because I was living life in two very different ways. I understood the concept of self-discipline and somehow I knew it was building within me a strong sense of integrity and good character, but I still didn't like working that hard.

Opelika is a small city, but in our little apartment we had everything we needed close by including several grocery stores, restaurants, and a mall. It was a totally different lifestyle than living out on grandma's farm. That lifestyle was something my peers in school knew nothing about. Most of them had never even seen cows or chickens. Yeah, they grew up playing outside, riding bikes, and doing a few chores—like washing dishes and taking out the trash, but they really didn't understand hard work like I did.

Early on, I hated going to the farm, because I knew I was going to have to work hard, and I didn't have to do that when I was living in our apartment in the little city of Opelika. Later I was thankful for all that hard work, I believe it helped me excel in sports and many other areas of my life.

I may not have embraced my farming foundation at first, and still to this day I have no desire to own a farm without a ton of help, but I have come to realize that growing up on our family farm instilled within me many invaluable lessons that extend far beyond the fields. Working together with my brother Terrell and my cousins Cicely and Antonio on that farm taught me teamwork. Living in a home built by the hands of my great, great-grandfather gave me a connection to my past, a sense of belonging and a little bit of understanding of the legacy and history of my family.

The shared meals around the table were moments of connection that reinforced the importance of family bonds. Learning to tackle tasks on my own built within me self-reliance. These experiences formed a solid foundation of values that have guided me through life.

I now embrace and appreciate my foundation which has provided a strong base from which to face challenges and pursue my goals with confidence and integrity. Now, I have an appreciation for teaching young children structure, responsibility, and hard work early in life, because it prepares them for adulthood and the hard work that will eventually manifest into whatever you set your mind to.

Your foundation may not be on a hard-working farm. It might be filled with struggles or triumphs. Whatever it is, it's vital that you embrace it. Your beginning whether good or bad shapes who you are. It provides many lessons that you will carry with you for the rest of your life. If you ignore or reject your foundation, you may have gaps in your own understanding of who you are.

By embracing your foundation and acknowledging it, you gain the strength and wisdom that comes from reflective growth. Even the hardest experiences teach us something. It may be resilience, perseverance, or a deeper appreciation of the path you're on now. Embracing your foundation, flaws and all, allows you to build something even stronger and more purposeful as you move forward in life. Own your story. Learn from it. Use your foundation for the platform to create your future.

# PRINCIPLE #2
## Take Pride in Your Name

---

*"A name represents the essence of a person's identity and character, and it carries the power to shape one's destiny."* —Unknown

---

One thing many people don't realize or understand is that names have meaning. Yes ... *your name* has a meaning.

Names carry energy and power through things like numerology. Numerology is the study of numbers and their special meanings, and in this belief, every letter of your name is connected to a number. (A = 1, B = 2, C = 3 and so on...) When you add up those numbers, they can tell you things about your personality, strengths, and even your life's purpose.

There are differences in how to calculate numerology depending on what dimension of your life the number is attempting to describe. Our human experience is very complex, so we have to look at each area of our lives in a different way. You will usually find different numbers for every area of your life. Here are some parts that I am familiar with:

- Soul Urge Number—focuses on your emotions and spiritual desires.
- Life Path Number—gives a broad overview of your life purpose and journey.
- Expression Number—shows your capabilities and potential.

- Personality Number—reflects how you present yourself and how you are perceived by others.

Every number is like a puzzle piece. When you put them together, you can see a picture of your true, full self and possibly even get a glimpse of your soul's journey.

The Soul Urge number for McKissic is Number 9. The Number 9 in numerology is a significant and profound symbol, representing the completion of a cycle. Through my studies, I have learned that people associated with the Number 9 are usually driven by a sense of fulfillment, are very dedicated to serving others, and have a deep connection to universal love.

For me, numerology says that I have psychic abilities, can carry on for others with joy, have a receptive nature that can carry burdens for others, am down-to-earth, thorough, strong-willed, practical and stubborn at times. It also says that I'm a hard worker, and often a martyr to duty. When I read this next part, I knew there was something to numerology: I like home and security above all, and I'm intuitive and probably interested in the arts, drama or science. To this whole assessment, I'll just respond, "YesSuhhhh!" Numerology got it right for me.

In addition to numerology, there is even more significance to our names. It's very important to take pride in our names because they represent us. Your name is a core part of your identity. Before we even enter a room, people see our names on applications, emails, and other documents. Whatever goes before you, you should be proud of it. When you aren't proud of your name or don't like it, that energy goes out before you and affects everything you do, even your confidence, in every part of your life.

When I was born, I took my mother's current last name, which was the last name of her ex-husband, the father of my older brother— McKissic, which is currently still my last name. My biological father's last name is Jordan. I didn't take his name because of some law in Alabama at that time. If the parents weren't married, they had to go through a bunch of loopholes for the child to receive the name of the father. So, my mother, of course, gave me her last name at that time. I'm sure she thought it would just be a temporary thing, and that she'd later go back and change it.

Fast forward to when I was around 10 or 11. My mother changed her name back to her maiden name, Smith, and asked me if I was interested in changing my last name to Smith as well. But in my pre-adolescent mind, I had already developed a sense of pride with my full name and had no issues with it. I was a kid and that seemed like a lot of work telling all my friends to start calling me something else. So, I said, "No, ma'am. I'll keep my name."

Before I fully understood the deeper significance and morality behind names, I experienced a pivotal moment when I was 17. During my senior year of high school, the patriarch of the McKissic family—my older brother's grandfather, Rev. Elijah McKissic, Jr.—invited me to his home. When I arrived, he took me aside and told me how proud he was of me. At that time, I had already received numerous offers for sports: around 27 for football, seven for basketball, and I was actively involved in community philanthropy. People were starting to recognize me as someone who might achieve great things one day.

He expressed his pride not just in my achievements but in how I represented his name and carried myself, both publicly and privately. His pride was also rooted in my role as an athlete and as a young man of faith, which resonated deeply with him as a pastor. He also instilled in me the importance of cultural and family heritage. You honor your ancestors and their past by how well you represent yourself in the present. When doing this, you are also setting up a legacy for anyone born after you with your name.

As I recall this memory now, after his passing, I realize how his words gave me that boost of confidence that I needed. So that when I walked into a room, I believed in myself, Jock McKissic. To this day because of him, I still have pride in who I am. He instilled in me a profound sense of pride in my name, shaping how I present myself to the world. As I've grown older and began studying the meanings behind names, I've discovered that my first name, Jock, means "God is gracious," while my surname, McKissic, carries its own significant meaning: *one who laughs and rejoices.*

These names now symbolize not only my personal beliefs and spirituality but also bring everything full circle. They remind me of the values I hold dear and the legacy I strive to uphold, reinforcing my pride in who I am and how I navigate the world.

With all of that said, I am going to let you in on a little secret. My given first name is JacQuez (pronounced Jah-Quez in the U.S.), It's not commonly pronounced that way in France when spelled that way of course. So, oftentimes people were confused on how to pronounce it. I did eventually change my name, professionally, to my lifelong nickname of Jock.

Taking pride in your name is more than a personal choice. It's a reflection of your identity, heritage, values, and aspirations. Names are not just labels we carry with us. Your name influences how you present yourself to the world and how you will contribute to the legacy of your name. People connect events to names. Make sure that when anyone hears your name whether they know you personally or not—it connects them to a good feeling or good memory, and you are setting the forces of good ahead of you wherever you go.

# PRINCIPLE #3
## Ice Cube, Carrot, Egg, or Coffee Bean

*"I never lose. I either win or learn."* —Nelson Mandela

I'm about to tell you a story that has left a lasting impression on me. It's a sort of parable about the concept of resilience and the different ways people respond to adversity. I hope this story helps you understand how your own responses to difficult situations can change the course of your life and others.

One day a young girl came to her mother and began complaining about everything that she was going through. "Mother, I'm so sick of dealing with adversity. Every time I turn around, I have something more to deal with. It doesn't matter what I do or how hard I try, I'm always coming up short."

She continued complaining as her mother listened. "Sometimes I feel like I just want to give up on life. I'm tired of believing in my goals. I've been working so hard and still I'm not even close to what I want. I'm ready to throw in the towel."

Her mother was a good listener and didn't say anything until the girl was finished complaining. They were sitting in the kitchen so it was no surprise to the girl when her mother calmly got up and took out four pots, filled each with water, and set them on the stove to boil. But when the mother started filling the pots with interesting ingredients, the girl became intrigued.

In the first pot she put several ice cubes. In the second pot she put only a couple of carrots, certainly not nearly enough for dinner. In the third pot she put a couple of eggs. And then in the fourth pot she put a few coffee beans.

The girl couldn't understand why her mother was doing this. She had never seen her cook like this before, "Mother, what on earth are you making?"

"In about 20 minutes you will see," replied her mother.

After 20 minutes passed, the girl's mother went over to the stove and turned off all the pots. Then she took out four bowls. She took some of the liquid from the first pot and put it in a bowl. Then she took the carrots from the second pot and put them in a bowl. She took the eggs from the third pot and put them in a bowl. Last, she took some of the liquid from the fourth pot and put it into the last bowl.

Placing all the bowls in front of her daughter, she said, "What do you see in the first bowl?"

"It looks like water."

The mother poured the contents into a cup, "Taste it," she said.

"Yeah, it's just water," the girl replied.

"What do you see in the second bowl?" asked the mother.

"Carrots."

"Touch the carrots."

"I think you cooked them too long. They turned to mush."

"You know what's in the third bowl. Eggs. Try cracking one of the eggs. Is the inside hard or soft?"

The girl hits the egg on the counter. The shell barely cracks. "You've cooked the eggs way too long. The inside is not at all soft anymore, no one will want to eat these eggs."

"We have one more bowl left," said the mother as she poured the dark liquid into a cup. "What do you see?"

"It looks like coffee," said the girl.

"Okay, taste it."

"Mmmm. Coffee," said the girl enjoying the drink. "But why all the other pots? What's the point?"

"All four different ingredients faced the exact same adversity, yet each one handled it very differently," said the mother. "The ice cube went into the boiling water, and it folded. Immediately turning into the environment surrounding it."

The mother continued with her lesson, "The carrots went in firm and strong, but when they faced the adversity of the boiling water they softened and weakened. The eggs, on the other hand, went in very fragile, their shells protecting the liquid inside, but when faced with adversity they became hardened."

The girl took another sip of the coffee as she listened closely to her mother.

"Now, let's think about the fourth pot. The coffee beans faced the same circumstances as all the other ingredients, but the coffee beans got better with adversity. Instead of allowing their surroundings to impact them in a negative way—they impacted their surroundings and turned it into something that is enjoyable for many people."

That story has stuck with me. I remember it every time I'm facing some kind of adversity. I have the option to choose how I'm going to "let" the adversity affect me, and how I'm going to come out on the other side.

If you liked this story, read the book by Damon West titled, *The Coffee Bean: A Simple Lesson to Create Positive Change*. Not only does he share the story but really goes deep into how your response can change you and your environment. Here is a short excerpt:

> The greatest growth and learning come from adversity. When we face challenges, we have the opportunity to become stronger and better. By choosing to respond positively to difficulties, we can turn them into opportunities for growth and transformation.

The coffee bean has the ability to change the water around it. It's not affected by the circumstances; instead, it changes them. You have the power to be the coffee bean, to rise above adversity, and to influence the world around you positively.

I am forever grateful to my former college coach, Dabo Swinney, for recommending that book to me many years ago. After reading it, I started looking at challenges and unpleasant circumstances in a different way. That book helped me start seeing the true power I had over my own life.

Many people are facing circumstances that may seem beyond their control. Yet even in the harshest conditions you have the power to choose your reaction. A perfect example of this can be found in another book, *Man's Search for Meaning,* by Viktor Frankl. This man survived some of the worst treatment known to humans while in a Nazi concentration camp. He says, "Everything can be taken from a man but one thing: the last of the human freedoms—to choose one's attitude in any given set of circumstances."

Choosing to impact one's surroundings while facing imprisonment is a profound example of resilience. Adversity can often push people to their breaking point. In the harshest of circumstances, many might be tempted to give in. However, it's crucial to remember that the power to shape our responses always lies within us.

When faced with severe challenges, a lot of people fold into their environment. Some will soften and give into weakness. Others will become hardened and refuse to allow themselves the true joy of living. The strength to endure and thrive comes from within. If we possess inner strength, unwavering faith, and a clear sense of who we are, we can confront, overcome, and muster up the courage to face any adversity. Then we'll come out even stronger than before.

# PRINCIPLE #4

## Lean Into Your Insecurities

---

*"I praise you because I am fearfully and wonderfully made; your works are wonderful, I know that full well." —Psalm 139:14*

---

Throughout my life, I've come to realize that many people are deeply insecure about their natural talents and gifts, especially when those abilities set them apart from their family members or peers.

One of the best artists I know is a family member (I'll refrain from whom). They can freehand almost anything they look at. But they aren't doing anything with that gift, well into their life.

Also, one of the best singers I've heard has yet to record one song, in fear of not being liked or building a fanbase.

These insecurities can cause people to hide their gifts. They will sometimes go out of their way to do the opposite of what they really want to do. They avoid exploring their talents, which could eventually lead them down the road to success and fulfillment.

But what causes insecurities, especially in relation to natural talents? Past experiences and trauma, comparison to others (aka Imposter Syndrome), setting unrealistic standards, lack of support or affirmation, fear of failure or rejection, negative self-talk, perceived weaknesses or flaws, unresolved relationships, to name a few.

The insecurities we feel about our natural talents are often rooted in unrealistic perceptions. While they may stem from past experiences or even trauma, these have little to do with the true, God-given gifts we possess. Sometimes, we create these insecurities by comparing ourselves to others (aka Imposter Syndrome) or by setting unrealistic standards for ourselves. Other times, they arise from a lack of support and affirmations, fear of failure or rejection, or even negative self-talk, just to name a few.

Unfortunately, this isn't just limited to talent. We can be insecure about physical traits too. Growing up, I experienced this firsthand. I was often teased about my height and my huge lips, and I developed insecurities about those things. I would slouch, trying to make myself smaller. I tried tucking in my lips because I was so self-conscious about them. In a sense I was trying to hide who I really was.

One day my Aunt Gloria Dubose noticed me walking with my head down and my shoulders hunched. She stopped me in my tracks and said, "Go back to the door and walk back toward me."

I did as she asked, still slumping and shuffling my way forward.

She shook her head and said, "No, stop." I looked at her, not understanding. She continued, "Now go back and do it again, but this time straighten your back and lift your chin. Then walk back to me again."

I felt awkward at first, but because I was taught to respect my elders I did as I was told. I walked toward her again, this time with my head held high and my shoulders back.

She smiled and said, "Doesn't that feel better?"

I smiled back and said, "Yes, ma'am it does." I was a little surprised by how a simple shift in my posture made such a change in the way I felt about myself.

"Exactly," she replied. "You only walk like that because you're insecure about yourself and you lack confidence. You really have no reason to be. Remember, you are perfectly made by God."

From that day on, any time I felt insecure about my physical features—or even my natural gifts and talents—I would hear her voice echoing in my mind reminding me to stand tall and embrace who I am, because I am perfectly and wonderfully made by God.

This lesson became a cornerstone in my life. It wasn't just about walking tall; it was about living tall, embracing all of who I am, even those things that I once thought of as flaws.

So many of us hide our gifts because we don't want to make the people around us uncomfortable. We subconsciously dim our light, afraid that shining too brightly will cast shadows on those who may not possess the same talents. I've seen it happen often, especially with people who grow up in families where their unique abilities stand out differently from those they love.

Imagine growing up in a house where no one can sing, but you have the voice of an angel. Instead of embracing that gift, you shy away from it. Then that energy overtakes you. If you are given the chance, you might get a feeling of stage fright or embarrassment, worried that you'll make the others around you feel inadequate. Or what about growing up in a family where everyone is talented and you spend your time comparing yourself to them? You are also talented, but you allow their talents to overshadow yours and you dim your light because you don't want to be compared to them feeling that they're so much better than you.

But here's the truth: every person has their own unique talents. We are all gifted in different ways, and none of us should feel the need to hide that. Instead, we need to lean into them. When we hold back or try changing what we really are, we aren't just doing ourselves a disservice, we're doing an injustice to the Creator who gave us those gifts in the first place. Each of us was made with intention, and the talents we have are meant to be used.

Failing to use our gifts is like telling God, "I don't really believe in the greatness you've placed within me. You've made a mistake or two when it comes to me." Can you imagine if Michael Angelo left his masterpiece hidden under a sheet, unseen and unappreciated. We not only cheat ourselves out of the fulfillment that comes from living authentically and fully embracing our strengths, but we cheat the world as well.

We were not made to shrink; we were made to expand. So, whether it's your height, your voice, your mind, or any other gift you've been blessed with, embrace it. Walk tall in who you are. Be proud of the person God made you to be. Stop worrying about whether your talents or appearance could make others uncomfortable. You are meant to share you with the world.

When we hide who we are, we deny the world the very thing it needs: our true, authentic selves. It's only when we embrace our gifts that we can live a life of purpose and fulfillment. So, if there's anything you've been holding back—whether it's a talent, a dream, or even just your own unique personality—now is the time to let go of those insecurities. Trust that you were made with intention, and that your gifts have a place in this world.

As my aunt told me, "You are perfectly made by God." And that's all the permission you need to be exactly who you are.

# PRINCIPLE #5

## Structure Your Day

---

*"The key to success is not just setting goals, but in structuring your day to make those goals a reality."* —Jim Rohn

---

Structure wasn't something that I understood or appreciated when I was a child. All I knew was that I was forced into it, and I had no say in it. Growing up, whether I was with my mom or my grandmother, Saturdays always started the same way. We would wake up, wash our face, brush our teeth—what they called "washing up"—and then eat breakfast. After that we would clean the entire house.

To be honest, I felt like the house was already clean because we were always made to keep things neat and tidy. My mom must've had a touch of OCD back then when it came to cleanliness, so the house never really got dirty in the first place. But still, every Saturday like clockwork, we scrubbed and polished. I didn't understand the point back then. I just knew it was part of our structure.

It wasn't until I started playing sports that I began appreciating the power of structure and routine. It was reiterated to us on a regular basis of why we needed structure. My coaches drilled it into us—why time management, schedules, and discipline were vital to success. During those summers in high school, we would work out at 5:30 A.M. every morning and be done by 7:30. This meant the rest of the day was ours to do whatever we wanted.

It was in these early mornings that I started to see how structuring my time could actually give me more freedom, not less. I'd come home after workouts, nap until about 10:30 or 11:00, and still have the entire day ahead of me. I could spend time with my friends—riding bikes, going to the pool, playing basketball, watching movies, or talking on the phone with my girlfriend. Whatever came up that day, I was ready to enjoy it.

I would have a full day, then I would come home and cook dinner for my mom before she got off of work or before she went to work (depending on her schedule). At that time, my mom worked third shift, so most of the time I cooked dinner before she left for work at 7:00 P.M. Afterward, I'd stay up watching TV and eventually crash around 10:30 or 11:00 P.M. Then the next morning I'd wake up again at 5:00 A.M. (exhausted beyond anything) you could imagine. My grandmother called it burning the candle at both ends.

After a few days of pushing myself too hard, I learned a crucial lesson: structuring my day wasn't just about squeezing more into it—it was about making sure I had the energy to enjoy it. I couldn't do everything under the sun every single day. That freedom was great, but too much of it without balance left me drained. By setting limits and finding balance, I could make the most of my time without running myself into the ground. Structure wasn't the enemy; it was actually the key to maintaining both discipline and freedom.

I found myself saying things like, "Oh, no. I'm not going swimming today, because I need to reserve some energy for tomorrow when we're running those 110 meter sprints or climbing those 18 hills." Even though I wasn't fully aware of what I was doing at the time, I was learning to structure my day. I wasn't writing anything down or thinking, "I'm going to do X, Y, Z … or I'm going to …. I was just subconsciously doing it because I didn't want to be exhausted when I woke up the next morning and started all the conditioning again. I learned to say no to things because in the back of my mind I could envision myself being dog tired, crawling up those hills the next day. So, I started structuring my day.

Then when I got into college, I consciously started doing it. Because of my tight schedule: 5:30 A.M. workouts, 7:30 A.M. study hall, 9:00 A.M. class, 11:00 A.M. class, lunch, another class, out of class by 2:00 P.M., go to the football facilities, watch a film, another workout practice, then shower, go home, get something for dinner, and by this time either go back to study hall, or go home and go to sleep because it's already about 9:30 or 10:00 P.M. The next morning, I would wake up and do the same thing all over again. Every moment counted. There wasn't a lot of room for error. In college I again was forced to be structured. I had no other choice if I wanted to play football and get good grades. I had to have a structured routine.

After graduating college and retiring from football a year and a half later, I moved to Atlanta to begin my acting career. It was then that I quickly realized how much less structured my life had become. Acting is such a sporadic thing. You never know when an audition opportunity will arise. For instance, as I'm writing this book, I've just received an email at 8:00 P.M. with an audition due tomorrow at noon. That goes to show how little structure there is to acting. This was especially true in the beginning of my career, because no one knew me yet, so there weren't as many chances to audition.

Unlike my previous experiences, where routines were clearly defined for me, in my acting career no one was forcing me to do anything. No one was telling me I needed to study, or practice, or watch a football film. I was free to do as I pleased, but after a couple months of this I began realizing just how important structure is in most successful people's lives, so I forced it upon myself. The responsibility of structuring my day now fell solely on me.

I realized how important structure could be to my future and my career. I needed to be ready at a moment's notice because I never really knew when the time would come when I would be competing for a role against someone in an unplanned cold read. I decided that over time good habits would pay off in the long run.

I forced myself to have a six o'clock wake up time. Then go to the gym, and then go to work, whatever odd job I was doing at the time. Then when I got off of my side gig, I would do something acting related for three hours. This time was spent studying TV shows or movies, sometimes watching interviews with actors or directors, analyzing plays, reading a bill from a play, or reading a script. It could be different every day, as long as I was doing something for three hours at the end of my day that would enhance my skills and knowledge as an actor.

That was my structure when I first started acting. By committing to this structured approach to life, I was not only honing my craft but also building good habits. Once I got to a place where I could (I won't say afford, because I really couldn't afford it at the time) make the money to pay for acting classes, I included classes in my routine. Sometimes I used the last of my meal money to pay for acting classes. But once I got the ability to make enough money to pay for acting classes, that became a part of the structure of my day, too. I knew I had to go to acting class on Monday, and then I would schedule a one-on-one with my acting coach, Dwayne Boyd, on a Thursday or a Friday. The further I got into my career, and I started booking roles, the more I realized that I would have to learn to pivot and change the structure of my day. The things that I planned were now being disrupted.

This is true not just for actors but for many people who have jobs that are not scheduled at the same time every day. Emergency workers, healthcare workers, reporters, journalists, and especially parents of young children. These people could have their day all planned out and then they get an emergency call, or the parent of a young child is teething and just needs to be held all day. The baby doesn't care that you have plans, he only knows what he needs. Even though interruptions are expected, everyone still needs a plan as to how they want the day to unfold. As the old saying goes, "Failing to plan—is planning to fail."

If you've put into place good habits and you've established a good structure to your day-to-day life, pivoting will be much easier when those unexpected things pop up. If there is something scheduled, do whatever you can to meet that promise; the other things can be shifted and set aside for now. Don't allow unforeseen events to throw off your entire day. Sometimes when something comes up out of the blue that isn't scheduled people think the day is ruined. No, the day is not ruined; the day has only changed.

For the people who have jobs that leave them little extra time, like me in my college days, having a structure to your day is vital because every second counts. Once Monday is gone, it's gone. There's no getting it back. You may not have any children or anyone disrupting your schedule, but your routine doesn't allow a lot of flexibility, so make sure those extra moments belong to you by making a plan and structure of what you want to fill them with. Make sure you add something you enjoy doing into your schedule. I call this *controlling the controllables*, which you'll read about in the next chapter.

The key is learning to pivot. Don't allow unexpected changes to throw off your entire day. There will always be commitments that must be kept, like a doctor's appointment, but for tasks that aren't time-sensitive, adjust according to the day's flow. Control the controllables and structure your day with this in mind. By doing so, you ensure that when your day shifts, you're still able to accomplish what needs to be done.

Don't get wrapped up in doing everything in a specific order. It's not about when you check things off your list, but that you do. You'll feel accomplished at the end of the day, no matter what order those tasks were completed. Structuring your day creates a sense of understanding and confidence. When you plan to succeed and complete what's set out for the day, you feel fulfilled. Even when life forces you to pivot, staying on top of tasks as they come ensures the world doesn't fall apart when something changes. You're still moving forward, and when things settle down, you're ready for the next challenge.

Making a decision and addressing whatever demands your attention becomes much easier when you've prepared and handled things well beforehand. On the other hand, if you're just winging it without a plan, unexpected challenges can feel overwhelming. You might find yourself thinking, "I haven't done anything, and now I have to do this" which can make the situation even harder to manage. That's why it's so important to stay on task and control the controllables.

# PRINCIPLE #6
## Control the Controllables

*"God, grant me the serenity to accept the things I cannot change, courage to change the things I can, and wisdom to know the difference."* —Reinhold Niebuhr

The prayer above is what control the controllables is all about. It's focusing on the things that you can actually do something about. A lot of people spend their time worrying about things they can't control. Remember the young girl in Principle #3 who complained and said, "I'm so sick of dealing with adversity"? She was not controlling the controllables. She was blaming the world for her problems.

For instance, as an entertainer, I want my agent to find auditions for me. Let's say I wake up, check my email, and start sulking because there is still no message from my agent. No auditions. No residual check on the way. Those are all things I have no control over, and my sulking would be me allowing that situation to control how I feel. If I were to stay in that mindset, those uncontrollables could ruin my entire day. But I have options: I can either continue sulking and have my whole day ruined or I can take control over my day with a different action that could lead me closer to my goal.

Growing up in the South, I noticed a lot of my elders struggled with controlling what they could actually control. They worried about everything, even things they had no control over. It was always, "I don't know how I'm going to handle this," or "I don't know what to do." And I would think, "Why are we worrying about something we can't change right now?" To me, it always seemed like common sense that if you can't change it, why waste energy on it? When I first heard the phrase "control the controllables," it just clicked for me.

If you can't change a thing physically, don't ever spend time worrying about it. Instead, focus on what you can control. How you spend your time, how you treat others, your attitude, these are things you can control and that shape your day and, ultimately, your future.

Charles R. Swindoll, a Christian pastor and author put it best when he said, "The remarkable thing is we have a choice every day regarding the attitude we will embrace for that day. We cannot change our past ... we cannot change the fact that people will act in a certain way. We cannot change the inevitable. The only thing we can do is play on the one string we have, and that is our attitude. ... life is 10% what happens to you and 90% how you react to it ... you are in charge of your attitude."

When it comes to control, many people—especially men—struggle because we often feel like everything has to go our way. We believe we must be in control of every aspect of our lives. This struggle is even more common among those who have experienced early success. Sometimes people think they're successful solely because of the actions they took, the decisions they made, or the steps they followed. This leads to a mindset of always trying to make the "right" decisions and create the "right" outcomes. Thinking that we reached this current position solely because of our own efforts and decisions. This mindset creates an unhealthy attachment to control, making it harder to accept that not everything is within our power.

While I fully support taking action and making good choices, it's important to remember that we've all had help along the way. No one can do it all on their own. Hanging on too tightly and trying to control everything and everyone can cause more harm than good—mentally, physically, and emotionally. Focusing on what you can control is far healthier in the long run.

And it's not just about protecting yourself, but also those around you. When you're overly concerned about controlling everything, it impacts the people in your life. Holding on too tightly to control can damage relationships just as much as it harms you. Trying to control every aspect of our lives can sometimes make us overlook the fact that there is a natural ebb and flow to everything. Life is filled with unpredictability and change. Seasons change, the weather fluctuates, and our personal and professional experiences are subject to forces beyond our control. If we're trying to control every detail, we risk missing the opportunities that arise from embracing uncertainty.

By letting go of the illusion of total control, we open ourselves to a more balanced way of living. I grew up around my grandma's and other family members' farms, so I saw a lot of uncontrollables. You do everything you're supposed to—planting, tilling, watering, and taking care of many other things. But then a drought hits and there's no rain for weeks. Or bugs infest the crops. Or deer eat and destroy them. Whatever the case, you always have the chance of losing some of your crops or cattle. A person could literally worry themselves to death over these uncontrollable things. Stress can be deadly when you're fixated on things you can't control.

So for me, if something unforeseen arises it's always about asking, "What do we do from here? How do we fix the problem? What do we still have to work with?" If it's something beyond our control—like an act of nature or God—then there's no point in stressing over it. You must pivot and focus on what you can do at this moment to make things a little better. You will never be able to change what has happened in the past.

Some people worry way too much over their past or future which steals moments from their present. In the movie, *Kung Fu Panda*,

Master Oogway gives us some good advice by saying, "Yesterday is history, tomorrow is a mystery, but today is a gift. That's why it's called the present." Think about what you can do in the present moment if your past or future seems to be getting you down.

I remember even as a child, I would fuss at my mom when she'd worry about things outside her control. The biggest culprit for her and many others is very often the past. So many people get stuck on what they did or didn't do, letting it affect them mentally in the present. But you can't control the past—it's already done. What you can control is what you do now. Learn from the past but focus on moving forward and making the right choices from here on out. This sets positive energy forces ahead of you.

If you find yourself hashing over the negative things you experienced in your day or any time in your past, Neville Goddard suggests you "… use the 'pruning shears of revision' on the events of the day, before you go to sleep, and revise them in your mind as you would like them to be, rather than as they were." Some people might say that means you're not facing the real world. It's not about escaping reality but rather about reshaping your mindset and emotional response to experiences.

Here's why this practice can be beneficial: you can reflect on what went wrong and envision a better way to handle similar situations in the future. By thinking about how you wish an event had unfolded, you can process your emotions and release any lingering negative feelings. This leads to improved mental well-being and reduces the impact of stress or disappointment. Additionally, visualizing a positive outcome can help you shift your perspective and focus on solutions rather than problems.

Control what you can. Don't worry about what you can't. Many times we can't control what is happening in our physical world but remember you can always control the way you think, the way you feel, the way you treat people, and of course, your attitude.

# PRINCIPLE #7
## Preparation Creates Swagger

---

*"It's not the will to win that matters—everyone has that. It's the will to prepare to win that matters."* —Paul "Bear" Bryant

---

Coach Holmes was my 7th grade basketball coach. He always used to say, "When you fail to prepare, you prepare to fail." At the time, it just seemed like a bunch of mumbo jumbo. I'd think, "Why does he keep saying that? Whatever, I don't want to hear it. Let's just get on to basketball." He was a very structured and methodical coach, and I had a lot to learn.

When I got to college, Coach Rumph, my defensive line coach, would say the same thing. And that's when it started to click for me. I began analyzing myself and my teammates. I noticed that the guys who were the most confident were the ones who worked extremely hard.

Looking back, I realized that for most of my sports career, I had been pretty confident, but I hadn't really connected the dots until college. I started noticing a pattern: in weeks when I missed something or didn't put in the extra effort, I wasn't as confident. I realized that it wasn't just in sports—it spilled over into every part of my life.

If I didn't study enough, I felt unsure about exams. If I didn't proofread a paper, I'd hand it in knowing it wasn't my best work. Even in my relationships—like when I didn't call my girlfriend enough during

## PREPARATION CREATES SWAGGER

a busy week—I'd notice problems creeping in, and she'd be upset. I understood subconsciously that I didn't feel nearly as confident when I wasn't prepared. That's when it hit me: *preparation* was the key to success in every phase of life.

I began understanding that I needed to focus on preparing to succeed. That meant not only doing what was required, but sometimes going a little above and beyond the requirements. Once I made preparation a habit, everything shifted. I started walking with a different energy, and people began noticing. I kept hearing things like, "You've got a lot of swag," and I thought to myself, "Yeah, man, that's because I work hard."

Now I began understanding why my coaches were driving in the principle of preparation. I felt good when I was prepared. I realized it wasn't just about confidence; it was because I had done the work, and I was ready. Like Vince Lombardi said, "The only place success comes before work is in the dictionary." When you've put in the effort, gone the extra mile, you've earned the right to be confident and have a little swagger.

But there's another side to this. We often beat ourselves up over the things we *didn't* do, rather than focusing on what we *did* accomplish. One little thing goes wrong, and we let it overshadow all the good we've done. It's like Winston Churchill said, "Success is not final, failure is not fatal: it is the courage to continue that counts."

For example, you might be three minutes late out the door, and suddenly you're thinking your whole day is ruined. You're beating yourself up because of things that you didn't do or didn't have time to do. Instead of thinking about all the things you've done right—studied, prepared, worked hard—and you're letting one small thing make you forget all the good. You have to remember to give yourself credit for the work you've put in. As long as you're prepared, things will be fine.

Focus on what you've been doing right. This helps you stay confident—and keep that swagger.

# PRINCIPLE #8
## Trust the Process

*"Many of life's failures are people who did not realize how close they were to success when they gave up."* —Thomas Edison

As I sit here thinking about the first time I truly trusted the process, it takes me back to when I learned how to tie my shoes. I can still remember all the steps: crisscross, bunny ears, loop, and pull through. At that moment, it felt like the hardest thing in the world. I remember thinking, *"There's no way I'll ever learn how to do this."* I couldn't imagine how other people had mastered it.

My younger cousin Ashley was with me, and although we were about the same age, she was a bit more confident. I remember her saying, *"You can do it."* That encouragement gave me the push I needed. Even though I didn't realize it at the time, I was learning to trust the process. I practiced again and again, and when I finally succeeded, I felt like the most accomplished little boy on earth.

That moment was my first real lesson in trusting the process. Over time, I've come to realize how important that lesson is in life. We all set out to accomplish things, and when we prepare for the steps we need to take, success usually follows. But too often, we get discouraged when things take longer than expected. Emerson tells us that, "Patience and fortitude conquer all things." Sometimes you just have to trust the process even though you don't understand how it's going to work. Losing faith in the process often leads to giving up right before the breakthrough.

You might only be three feet away from striking it rich like R.U. Darby and his uncle (you can read the story in Napoleon Hill's book, *Think and Grow Rich*). They staked a claim during the gold rush and began digging, hoping to strike it rich. After weeks of hard work, they discovered a vein of gold and were able to sell a little. But the gold vein eventually ran dry, and it seemed like there was no more gold to be found.

Darby and his uncle were sick of the mining process that was producing little or no reward. They were frustrated and discouraged. Giving up on their dreams of gold, they sold their mining equipment to a junk dealer for a small amount of money and left the mine behind.

Then the junk dealer began wondering if maybe Darby and his uncle didn't give the process a good enough chance. He thought maybe there really was gold in the mine, so he brought in an expert to study the mine and learned that Darby stopped digging—are you ready for this— just three feet away from one of the richest veins of gold in the entire state.

Of course, the junk dealer capitalized on this knowledge and went on to make a fortune from the mine while Darby learned a valuable lesson about not quitting when faced with temporary defeat. He learned to trust the process. He promised himself to never again give up on something and lived by this lesson. He went on to become one of the top sellers in the life insurance sales industry.

What's helped me keep faith in the process in everything I have done and in everything I do is identifying examples of others who I respect that have already walked the path that I'm now walking. Whether it was becoming a good starter on the varsity football team, making a certain grade on the ACT, becoming a successful college player, getting my college degree, or even becoming an actor, I found someone who had already done well what I was attempting to do and worked with them.

In high school it was my "big brother" Tommy Jackson, a former teammate of mine. In college it was my teammate, Gaines Adams (rest in peace). Then there was Arnold Schwarzenegger, initially, when it came to acting. I decided if he could move from Austria to America and not even have English as his first language, surely I could do it too. I always looked to people who left behind a blueprint for me to use as an example of how to trust the process and move forward. This gives you a sort of visual perspective.

Too often people pray for something they want, but they don't take into consideration the size of the thing they're praying for or what they must become before receiving it. You may need to put in a lot of self-work before you're even ready to accept it.

I have a vision of becoming one of the greatest actors to ever live, but I also know that isn't going to happen in five or ten years. It takes time, work, dedication, and a willingness to face challenges. I didn't go into acting thinking, *"If this doesn't work out in a decade, I'll move on."* I am committed to it for life, no matter how long it takes. I trust the process.

I knew that this thing I prayed for and desired was going to take X amount of work. When I say, "X amount," it's because I don't know the exact figure; I just know it's going to require a lot. So, the only thing I can do is trust the process. When you trust the process, you find it easier to weather the storms. It all becomes part of the plan.

When you lose sight of the process—when you stop trusting it—that's when you start to question yourself, your progress, your worth, and whether you're cut out for whatever it is you're pursuing.

Recently, I passed my real estate exam for California. I've always had a desire to be a real estate investor. Once I reach a certain point in my career and have the funds, I plan to invest. About two years ago, I thought, "Why not start from the agent side to learn that aspect as well?" So, I enrolled in a real estate class. It was extremely difficult and something I wasn't familiar with, despite my love for houses. *H.G.T.V. is probably my biggest secret—my favorite channel!* When people ask what no one knows about me, that's it. I know what I like, but as far as the laws and regulations, all of that was foreign to me.

I took my test the first time, needing a score of 70 to pass. I scored a 68—just two points shy. When I took it again, I scored a 67, which felt like going backward. Doubt crept in, and the human side of me thought, "I don't know if I can do this." But I caught myself because I had so much skin in the game, I knew I had to trust the process, so I committed to studying again, determined to pass. That moment of trust was pivotal. The very next time I took the exam, I passed! Now, a couple of months later, I'm ready to get started.

In every phase of life, we must remember to trust the process. Have faith in yourself, in the process, and in God to help you keep going. I believe in you—you can do it. You can make your dreams come true by trusting the process.

# PRINCIPLE #9
## Find a Hobby

*"Make time for your hobbies. Your mind, body, and spirit will thank you for it."* — Unknown

The reason I chose "hobby" as one of the principles is because I didn't really understand the importance of having a hobby as an adult until maybe 2016. Before that, I was living in Atlanta, acting, and working to move up the acting ranks. I've never had a career job or used my degree. I've always taken on various jobs like security, driving limos, and marketing—whatever came up—because I wanted flexible work that allowed me to attend auditions or take on acting roles whenever they came up.

I graduated with a double major in Communications and Sociology, which helped me as an actor, but I never tried to get a job in those fields. I took on these gig jobs to stay free for auditions or set work. I could just say, "Hey, I'm not coming tomorrow," and they'd be like, "OK, we'll get someone to fill in." But because those jobs paid so little, I found myself working all the time. If I wasn't on set, I was pretty much working. I'd get off of work, maybe go to acting class, hit the gym, go home, shower, and sleep. Then I'd wake up and do it all over again. It was starting to feel a bit like *Groundhog Day*.

I wasn't doing anything for myself, I wasn't dating or doing anything fun outside of acting. One day I realized how mentally exhausted I was when I heard someone talking about their hobbies. They said something like, "Oh, I go bowling every Thursday, and my girlfriend and I go hiking on Sundays." That stuff sounded fun.

I started replaying my life. I took a long, hard look and asked myself, "What am I doing for fun? What are my hobbies?" I realized I had none. So, I made a bargain with myself to start with something that would add to the craft of acting. I had to do something so that I was no longer stuck in a time loop.

I made a promise to myself to go to the movies every Tuesday—that would be my hobby. So, I started going every week. Then I began noticing that on Wednesdays, I was more energized. The brain fog was gone, and I was nicer. Not that I was unpleasant before, but I just felt jollier and more upbeat. I realized that taking time for myself and finding a hobby made a huge difference. This was around 2016 or 2017. Since then, I've made it a point to have hobbies and take time for myself, doing something I enjoy at least once a week that has nothing to do with work.

These days, I still go to the movies, sometimes twice a week. Now that I'm more successful in my field and have more control over my schedule, I have more time to do things I enjoy. In 2020, I got into cycling when everything was closed, and gyms were shut down. I had to find a way to stay fit and work out. So, I bought a bike and fell in love with riding—I felt the freedom it gave me like when I was a child riding with my friends around our neighborhoods.

During COVID, I went home to be with my family and started riding every day. Then a friend of my mom's who had a cycling bike (also known as a road bike) said to me one day, "Hey, you should try riding my road bike."

I looked the bike over. It had a really light frame ... thin tires. It was built for speed. It was the kind of bike you see riders using in the Tour de France.

I smiled at him and said, "Nah, I think I weigh too much for that bike."

He kindly debunked that theory and convinced me to give it a try. I couldn't believe how fast and smooth it was. It made riding much easier. After that, I was hooked. The very next week, I went out and bought my own road bike. I totally fell in love with cycling. It not only became a passion but also made me healthier.

I always tell people that health is wealth and taking care of yourself is crucial. Many people who don't have an athletic background find it hard to go to the gym. So, I encourage people to find a physical hobby they enjoy, whether it's walking, hiking, biking, or skating, whatever it is you enjoy. It's a great way to stay active while doing something you love. This way, like the old saying goes, you can kill two birds with one stone. Something enjoyable and physical.

Many different studies and experts agree that we need to find time for something other than work. Chris Bailey actually conducted a year-long experiment on productivity. He spent that time testing many different theories and eventually wrote a book called *The Productivity Project.* In his writing, he emphasizes that hobbies not only provide relaxation but also serve as productive breaks that rejuvenate your mental energy. He states, "Habitual tasks [or hobbies] not only give our mind a rest from the demands of work and life, but they also help us unearth insights while we plan for the future."

Sabine Sonnentag, a professor of organizational psychology, tells us that regularly detaching from work is important for stress recovery and creativity. In her research, she found that even taking a short vacation or weekend getaway leads to long-term productivity. In her studies she also found that pursuing "mastery activities" or hobbies when you're not at work can be extremely helpful, saying that engaging in enjoyable, skill-building activities plays a key part of improved work performance.

In today's society, many of us are constantly caught up in the same routine, always moving from one task to the next. Taking a break to engage in a hobby allows us to reset, to pause and reflect on what truly matters. It's a moment to step away from the busyness of life and recognize all the blessings in our lives. By taking that time, we not only recharge but also create space to thank God for our health, our abilities, and all that we have. It's in those quiet moments of doing something we love that we can reconnect with ourselves and be grateful for the life we've been given.

If you want to reduce your stress level and improve your performance at work, become the master of your life and take up something that you enjoy doing. If you take up a physical hobby your mind, body, and boss will thank you.

# PRINCIPLE #10
## Create a Fun Workout Routine

*"Physical fitness is not only one of the most important keys to a healthy body; it is the basis of dynamic and creative intellectual activity."* —John F. Kennedy

Discovering a workout routine that's *fun* (emphasis on *fun*) is especially true for people who didn't grow up with an athletic background or weren't in situations where working out was built into their routine. For those individuals, going to a physical gym or running three miles around the neighborhood might not feel like the most enjoyable thing to do. That's why exploring different activities that spark interest is imperative.

I started playing organized sports in middle school, in seventh grade. By ninth grade, I joined the football and basketball teams. That's when our coaches began providing structured workout routines. We worked out daily during the school year, and in the summer, we trained every morning, five days a week.

Things shifted when I started playing professionally in arena football. Unlike before, we weren't required to work out, but by that point, it was embedded in me to maintain a high level of physical activity—not just for my athletic performance but for my overall health and even my mental well-being. Working out was good for my mind. So, I did it. From the year 2000 until 2010—a solid 10 years—I was playing organized sports and working out consistently.

## CREATE A FUN WORKOUT ROUTINE

The moment I retired, I promised myself I wouldn't go to the gym for a year. After spending 10 straight years being forced to work out—I needed a break. I don't know if I made it the full year, but I did go several months without stepping into a gym. Eventually, I started working out again, it had become part of my DNA. This time I wasn't working out for a football game or a season, but for my own personal health benefits. I knew what Jim Rohn said was true, "Take care of your body. It's the only place you have to live." However, I realized my relationship with the gym had changed. It felt different—almost jaded. I knew at that point I needed to find some fun, new, interesting, and entertaining ways to stay active.

I began exploring alternatives, like band exercises, rope workouts, and machines like elliptical. I started incorporating yoga and cycling—activities I had never tapped into before but found genuinely interesting. Doing these things made it much easier to work out regularly. I wasn't just forcing myself into a routine; I was looking forward to trying something new.

There are countless ways to implement exercise without it feeling like a workout. You could walk your dog for three miles, play with your toddler at the park by actively chasing a ball, throwing a frisbee, or even flying a kite. You could go roller skating, skateboarding, or swimming laps at a community pool. The key is finding what excites you. There are so many fun ways to get out and move to keep yourself active, but you have to explore and try different things to see what piques your interest. Once you find it—it will no longer feel like a mandatory workout and will feel fun and enjoyable.

When you explore different activities, you might discover something that turns exercise from a chore into a treat. You want the thought of working out to be a reward, not something hanging over your head. When you wake up in the morning and your feet hit the ground, you want to feel that spark of excitement—knowing you *get* to move your body in a way that makes you happy.

Find the time to explore what works for you. Find activities that keep your body healthy, your mind clear, and your spirit lifted. Exercise isn't just about physical fitness; it's about maintaining mental and emotional well-being, too. Studies show that activities like running, cycling, or swimming not only improve cardiovascular health but also boost mood by releasing endorphins, reducing anxiety, and enhancing cognitive function. Regular aerobic activities are also associated with better sleep and decreased symptoms of depression.

In the morning when you wake up and your feet hit the floor, you want to be excited about your day. It should never feel heavy and like a chore. Actress Rakul Preet Singh from Bollywood is the owner of three *F45 Training* facilities. She says, "For me, fitness is not just about hitting the gym; it is also about an inner happiness and an overall well-being." This statement highlights the deeper purpose behind staying active—it's not just about physical results but about feeling joyful, balanced, and healthy.

When it comes to making fitness a fun and integral part of your life, the advice is simple: find what you love and run with it. (No pun intended.) Whether it's dancing to your favorite music, trying a new group class, or discovering an outdoor activity like hiking or biking, the key is to enjoy what you're doing. Remember, the best workout is the one that brings a smile to your face while keeping you healthy at the same time. Fitness can be a celebration of life, energy, and happiness—and fun!

# PRINCIPLE #11
## Remain Curious

---

*"Curiosity is the wick in the candle of learning."*
—William Arthur Ward

---

Remaining curious is important because it applies to multiple facets of life. It's key to becoming successful in any industry. It's also important for building genuine friendships, relationships, and more.

Another reason to stay curious is it helps you to be authentic to yourself because it encourages exploration and openness to new ideas and perspectives. Curiosity pushes you to question your beliefs, reflect on your values, and learn from different experiences. By constantly seeking to understand more about yourself and others, you avoid falling into narrow and automatic patterns of thinking. This keeps you connected to your true authentic self. By staying curious, you make choices that feel right for you, instead of doing things just to fit in or meet others' standards.

If you want to have good relationships, it's extremely important to remain curious about the people who are most important to you in your life. Most people don't even consider this, because we're all so caught up in our own lives. Staying curious in personal relationships helps you stay engaged and opens the doorway to learning more about the people you care about. You do this by actively listening to what they are saying and doing. This will deepen your understanding of them and allow you to appreciate their thoughts, feelings, and ever-changing experiences. When you remain curious, you're less likely to make assumptions or take things for granted. Staying curious fosters stronger communication, trust, and deeper emotional connections. When you show a person genuine interest, you may be surprised how much it strengthens the bond between you.

Whenever you show curiosity about someone, even if it's only in a brief conversation, it can make them feel valued and respected. It demonstrates that you're genuinely interested in who they are and what they have to say. This can build trust and mutual respect. People appreciate it when others take the time to listen to their thoughts and experiences. This creates a positive impression and helps them feel seen and understood. No matter how brief an interaction you have with someone, if you are kind enough to be curious (even if it's only a short or one-time conversation) it can lead to a lasting, positive impact on their lives.

Many times when we meet others, we don't really dive into who they are or where they come from. For me, I've always been curious, but mostly I'm an observer, watching and listening to people—that's been my nature for pretty much my whole life. I started doing security and it became an even bigger part of who I was because as a security guard you don't talk—you just observe.

Then I read this book by a phenomenal film producer, Brian Grazer. He's one of the most successful producers in history. A lot of producers play it safe, sticking to only what they know from experience. If you're an Italian producer, you produce Italian movies. If you're a Black producer, you produce movies that highlight the Black culture and people. But Brian Grazer has produced an incredible range of films across various cultures and countries. For example, *A Beautiful Mind* (American intellectual), *The Missing* (Native American culture), *The Da Vinci Code* (Italian Culture and history), *Restless* (British culture).

He's a white guy who's also produced major blockbuster Black films like *Boomerang, CB4, The Nutty Professor, LIFE,* and *American Gangster.* These are films that are deeply connected to our culture. Most people would never guess that he produced them.

He has done so many different types of movies, but what made me want to read his book was after I saw him in an interview. He was asked, "How do you produce films from cultures so far removed from your own?" He said, "I just found a way to remain curious." That stuck with me, so I read his book *A Curious Mind*. It inspired me to shift from just observing people to actively engaging with them by asking questions, learning more, and guiding conversations.

Now, I am genuinely curious about what's going on in the minds of others, what their lives are like and where they come from. When you remain curious and open to conversation, you learn so much about the world. You discover that, even though we all look different on the outside, we ultimately all have an array of similarities.

Brian Grazer says at one point he was interviewing three or more people from different walks of life every week. Today, he's done around 2,000 interviews. He talks to everyone, from sanitation employees to doctors and anesthesiologists. Since reading his book, I've become more interested in engaging with people who don't look or talk like me, who come from different backgrounds. This has made me more successful as an actor because I now have more experiences and stories to draw from. It has also improved my own personal relationships.

Many people, especially men, can go through life without having deep conversations, even with their significant others. It's not personal; it's just that we don't always have anything we want to talk about. That's how God wired us. Some men can go through life without having any heartfelt discussions, often just exchanging casual greetings. We exist more through our actions than our words, and this isn't a lack of interest. It's just how we were created. It tends to be innately who we are. Most women, on the other hand, are by nature nurturers—it's part of who they are to ask questions and make sure everyone is feeling okay.

    I always tell women that if he loves you and is present, you don't have to worry about his communication style. Even though I'm curious, sometimes I'm still very quiet. Every once in a while I'll hear a woman say, "You don't talk much." I'll reply, "Yeah." She'll say, "Sometimes I feel like I'm doing all the talking." I explain, "It's just how God designed me as a man. I tend to be more of an observer." Then I tell her, "If you ask a question, I'll give you all the answers you want, but most men don't volunteer information." It's not a bad thing; just ask a question, and you might get a dissertation in response. Some men talk a lot because of how they were raised, their foundation and personality from what they observed. Other men stick to the DNA ingrained in them, which often means not talking about things, just observing their surroundings and staying quiet and focused.

    I have learned, however, that staying curious in my relationships strengthens bonds and connections because I know what is going on in my loved ones' lives. I ask people about their dreams and goals. This has not only helped my personal relationships, but even my interactions with strangers. Most people want to talk about themselves. They rarely get the chance. I've made it a point to create that opportunity for them.

    In the South, sometimes people will say, "That boy's been here before," referring to me. This typically means that the person exhibits wisdom or a kind of familiarity with life that seems beyond their years. It suggests that the individual has an old soul, implying they carry insights or experiences that are often associated with someone who has lived longer or has encountered significant life lessons. It reflects the mindset I'm meant to embrace, so I give credit where it's due, it's because I'm a curious observer.

# PRINCIPLE #12
## Tons of Accountability and a Dose of Grace

*"I think the most important thing is to be consistent. You've got to be accountable, and you've got to understand your limitations, but you've also got to be patient with yourself."* —Tim Duncan

Many people weren't taught accountability as children. Maybe their parents did everything for them, or when they messed up, they weren't held responsible and their parents let them off the hook easily. As adults, they often struggle with accountability because it was ingrained in them to avoid taking responsibility. Some people who have grown up without ever having to be responsible may want to hold themselves accountable, but they are still battling what they subconsciously learned as a child. They were never taught the importance of choices and decisions.

If you were never expected to maintain a certain standard of ethics or responsibility growing up, it can lead to a mindset of blaming others—whether it's teachers, bosses, or even friends—rather than owning up to your mistakes. As Benjamin Franklin once said, "A man who is good at making excuses is seldom good at anything else."

It's especially evident in younger generations like Gen Z, who grew up in an era when everyone received a trophy just for participating. This idea, though well-meaning, can subconsciously teach kids that effort isn't necessary to succeed. However, when they enter the workforce or start a business, reality sets in quickly—there are no trophies for halfhearted efforts, and failure is often met with disappointment or even loss of opportunity.

Much of this stems from my generation, who are now parents. We're softer on our kids than our parents were, giving them more leeway. When everybody gets a trophy—everyone wins. Subconsciously this teaches children: 'If I don't do my best or win, I still win.' But the moment you graduate high school, college, or start a job or business, you quickly learn that blaming others doesn't work. It doesn't matter how many times you complain, it's not going to help. It does no good blaming your situation on others, "I didn't get the contract because they're more attracted to the other person." No, you didn't get it because your proposal wasn't good enough, and you should've worked harder.

For me, it was different. I was raised to be held accountable. From a very early age I had to keep my room clean, maintain good grades, and take on real responsibilities. My mom and grandmother taught me how to cook when I was very young. By the age of 13 I was in charge of preparing meals when my mother worked third shift. She would go into work around 7:00 P.M. and get off at 7:00 A.M. She told me, "I've taught you how to cook and clean. You gotta help me out here—do what you gotta do." So, I would cook dinner and breakfast, but on her days off she would cook for me.

Many people overlook the importance of creating a balanced exchange of responsibilities between parents and children in the home. Helping children learn essential life skills builds mutual respect within the family. When both parents and children are involved in household duties, it teaches children the importance of contributing to the family and gives them confidence in themselves.

Experts say giving children responsibilities at a young age helps develop important life skills. Children who are assigned age-appropriate tasks, such as chores, develop a sense of competence, accountability, and self-confidence. It encourages independence and builds strong work ethics. Research shows that children who have responsibilities at home are more likely to develop better problem-solving skills, emotional regulation, and a greater understanding of consequences, which prepares them for future responsibilities in school and adulthood.

When I started driving, my mom gave me even more responsibilities; she entrusted me with balancing the checkbook and paying the bills. She was kind and patient as she taught me to read the bills, subtract them from the total in her bank account, and how to write the check. Then I would go pay the bill. I knew she wasn't going to make excuses for me if I failed to pay the electricity bill—it was my responsibility, and if the lights got cut off, that was on me … not her. The responsibilities I was given weren't just about doing chores; they showed me how to take ownership of my actions, no matter the outcome. She was teaching me to become a man.

There's something else here that needs to be mentioned. I knew my mom trusted me and I didn't want to let her down. When a parent fully truly trusts a child and the child truly understands this trust, something magical happens. It boosts the child's self-esteem, making them feel valued and competent, capable of handling challenges. The child begins to understand that their actions really do matter, but most importantly that Mom, Dad, Grandmother … are trusting and depending on me and believe I can do this, and I don't want to let them down.

In contrast, if a parent believes the child is likely to fail, it can diminish the child's self-worth and discourage them from trying. Trust empowers children to step up to challenges and rise to the occasion, while doubts from a parent about the child's ability often result in a lack of motivation and increased fear of failure. Positive reinforcement through trust builds resilience, accountability, and a stronger belief in one's own potential.

I am extremely grateful to my mother and grandmother for making me accountable when I was young. The older I got the more I could see just how these skills of being responsible were helping me in my life. When I became an athlete the reason for being responsible for one's own actions became clear. Even though you're working together as a team, everyone has to be personally accountable to maintain a certain level and to do their best during the game. If one person isn't prepared and falls short, it can mean losing instead of winning.

That means if I didn't perform, I had to run extra laps or do additional drills. In athletics, as in life, you quickly learn that when you fall short, it's on you to fix it. That mindset prepared me for the workforce and entrepreneurship, where you're held accountable whether you like it or not. The moment you start pointing fingers, you've already lost ground because you're taking two steps backward.

Whenever something goes wrong for me now and then, I don't blame others. Instead, I look in the mirror and ask myself, "Okay, what did I do … what didn't I do … to make this situation blow up in my face?" Then I analyze it and ask myself, "What can I do to make this situation better now?" That kind of self-reflection is crucial because it helps me see where I went wrong and how I can improve for the future. Accountability is about looking inward first, before pointing outward. It's about owning your failures as much as your successes, and through that process, becoming better.

Sometimes things can happen that are truly out of our control. Maybe a teacher gave you the wrong assignment, your boss texted the wrong address, or your proposal was good, but a PDF glitch messed it up. Once you assess the situation and figure out what you did or didn't do, you need to give yourself grace. Be honest and say, "I did my best here, here, and here, but this one thing happened that I couldn't control—it wasn't my fault." It's important to give yourself grace, recognizing that you did all you could do in this situation, and it just wasn't meant to work out this time.

If there are places where you went wrong once you identify the issue, make a promise to yourself to improve. This gives you control over your own life. When you cast blame, you are giving others control. So, own up to your mistakes—that's your accountability—then you have to let it go and give yourself grace. You can't hold on to mistakes. Accountability and grace go hand in hand.

# PRINCIPLE #13

## Forgiveness

*"Be kind to one another, tender-hearted, forgiving one another, as God in Christ forgave you."* —Ephesians 4:32

I think forgiveness is such an important principle, not just for others, but for our own well-being. It's often overlooked, even though it's crucial. People go through life wronging one another—we're not perfect. And we hold on to grudges without even realizing it because it becomes a part of life, and we think it's normal. For example, if you step on my toe today and I don't see you again for two weeks, I might still remember that you stepped on my toe and didn't apologize. It sounds small, but I've seen it happen. I've witnessed people holding on to even larger wrongs, and often the other person doesn't even know they've done something wrong.

Now, there are occasions when someone does something out of spite, and they know it, and they know you're upset with them. But in many cases, when people wrong us, they don't realize how it has affected us. Too often, we go through life holding on to grudges for no reason. There's a quote that has been attributed to both Nelson Mandela and Buddha, "Resentment is like drinking poison and waiting for the other person to die." That sums it up so perfectly, because that is what happens whenever you choose holding onto a grudge over forgiveness. It doesn't affect the other person involved nearly as much as it does you.

Even if someone wronged you out of spite, they move on with their day and most likely forget all about you. For example, if someone cuts you off in traffic, and you're yelling and screaming, they're probably on the phone, talking about business, unaware that you even exist. You stay angry for hours, but they're at home cuddling with their wife. We go through life holding on to these cups of poison, drinking them (sometimes savoring them), waiting for the person who wronged us to suffer.

But forgiveness isn't for them; it's for you. Most of the time, you're the one suffering from what they did. We've all heard the saying, *forgive but don't forget*; too many people focus on the "don't forget" part. They claim to forgive but keep bringing up the wrong, which isn't true forgiveness. Yes, we have brains, so we might remember things, but we don't have memories of elephants. If we truly forgive, we don't hold on to the hurt.

No matter what religion or non-religion you are, Ephesians 4:32 is a good motto to pattern your life: *Be kind to one another, tender-hearted, forgiving one another, as God in Christ forgave you.* Think about how people wronged Christ—they killed him. If God can forgive us, how can we live among each other and not forgive each other for small mishaps? Think of the words of the Messiah when they were crucifying him, "Father forgive them. They know not what they do." People often act without intention, and we have to recognize that.

In the most popular prayer in the world, *The Our Father* or *Lord's Prayer*, there's a line about forgiveness that is very profound: *forgive us our trespasses as we forgive those who trespass against us.* I've been saying this prayer since I was about four years old. My great-grandmother, Ezella "Mama E" Moffett—may she be remembered—sat me down in a rocking chair and had me repeat it until I learned it. So, I've been saying it for 34 years, but that line, *forgive us our trespasses as we forgive those who trespass against us,* didn't really hit me until a minister whom I am very close to broke it down for me.

"What does that mean to you?" asked my dear friend and mentor Prophet Jones.

I gave the basic answer, "God forgives me as I forgive others."

Then he said, "Say it again."

At that moment I realized—how many people, who are devout believers, say this prayer but don't truly grasp it. If you're not forgiving others, can you expect God to forgive you? A lot of times, we hold on to hate and grudges, and when things aren't going right in our lives, we blame someone else because of it. But really, we're not being accountable when we do this, because we're not forgiving. And because we're not forgiving, God isn't forgiving us. It's causing turmoil in our lives, and we're being locked out of God's will because we're holding on to hate.

The biggest example of this in my life was learning to forgive my biological father, who left me and my mom when I was around six months old. I didn't have a real conversation with him until I was 36 years old. In college, I said a prayer, telling myself that I forgave him, but when he came back into my life, all the feelings I had as a child resurfaced. That's when I realized I hadn't truly forgiven him. I just assumed he wouldn't come around again, so I wouldn't have to face the fact that he wasn't there when I was growing up. I wouldn't have to confront him with how much my mom struggled because of his absence.

Once I faced the fact that I hadn't forgiven him, I decided to call him and verbally tell him that I forgave him. I'll never forget that moment on the phone when I told him I forgave him. It was the moment I realized I had been holding onto that hurt for 36 years. I also felt and heard his relief when he heard me say it.

I felt like a weight had been lifted. I felt so relieved. I had no idea I'd been carrying that burden for so long. Even though I forgave him, we still don't really have much of a relationship and that's okay. He's sick now, and when he first reached out, it was because he thought he wasn't going to live much longer. He's in and out of the hospital every other month or so. And that was another reason why I felt it was important to forgive him before he transitions. He has nine kids—one passed away earlier this year—but *I* was the only one who had no relationship with him.

The whole human race, for the most part, tends to look at how the situation affects them personally. We rarely consider what the other person(s) involved could be feeling. I never considered that my biological father could be carrying guilt but heard his relief when I forgave him.

I've thought a lot about it, and while I don't know all the specifics of why he left, he did tell me that he didn't value family the way he should have. I think it's deeper than that. We often tell ourselves that if our mom or dad had been there, things would have been better, things would have been different. But just because someone is present doesn't mean they're truly present. Sometimes, their presence could make things worse. Sometimes the presence of a person in your life can be truly detrimental. If my dad had stayed, I don't think I'd be where I am today. People sometimes tend to hold onto their pain, thinking about what could have been. Yet everything that happens to us shapes us into who we are today. And that's another reason to forgive, even for something as deep as your mom or dad leaving. Those hurts can shape you in ways you might not even realize.

The Bible says, "Your ways are not my ways," and I truly believe that. Even though we think our parents should have been there, or that our spouse shouldn't have left, or _____ fill in the blank … should have done it this way …. There's a bigger plan in play. It's not always for us to understand at the time. What we do need to understand is that forgiveness frees us—allowing us to live the life we were truly meant to live, unencumbered by any past hurts and broken promises. Leave the things that don't serve you now in the past by forgiving, so that you can live in the future in peace.

# PRINCIPLE #14
## Give a Little to Get a Little

---

*"You give but little when you give of your possessions. It is when you give of yourself that you truly give."*
—Kahlil Gibran

---

Even though this principle can be applied to everything in our lives, let's begin with a little R-E-S-P-E-C-T to quote the famous Aretha Franklin. Respect in its most basic form is about recognizing the value and dignity of others, regardless of status or circumstance. Most of us want to be respected, but we don't always think about how much respect we're giving to others. I'll include myself in that because I've been guilty of it too. We often fail to be mindful of the respect we're offering.

A lot of times people try to demand respect. Thinking to themselves, "If you respect me, I'll respect you." But what if respect started with you, and you were the first one to give a little respect? The moment you offer respect, it's usually returned. Instead of two people in a room having a standoff about who's going to be respectful, you can break that barrier by making the first move.

The concept of "give a little to get a little" can extend to almost every aspect of life. Everything in life is connected to this idea of giving. Anything that has energy requires a bit of give and take. It's all about reciprocation. Often, relationships—whether they are friendships, partnerships, or even professional connections—can become lopsided.

One person may be giving their all, while the other is contributing little or nothing. Some people might tolerate this imbalance for a while, but not for long. Eventually the relationship will most likely dissolve if there is not some sort of give and take from both sides.

In the Bible, Yahshua (Jesus) taught us the Golden Rule: Do unto others as you would have others do unto you. That's pretty straightforward, easy to apply, and to understand, but if I find myself constantly doing things for you while you do nothing in return, eventually that cycle will break. I'll reach a point where I stop giving altogether. Genuine relationships thrive on mutual effort and understanding. It doesn't always have to seem fair on both sides—reciprocation isn't always identical energy, just some sort of give and take.

My business partner and close friend, Brock Lawrence, lives by a code from a quote that I've come to embrace into my own life: "Treat the janitor with the same respect as you do the CEO." I've witnessed him live out this principle day after day. Many people will adjust their behavior and their level of respect depending on someone's title or status, but Brock continues to show unwavering respect for everyone, regardless of their role or job in life. True integrity is shown through how we treat everyone we meet, even those that society often overlooks. Character isn't measured only by how we interact with those who have power, but how we honor every individual.

In *Life's Little Instruction Book*, H. Jackson Brown, Jr. says, "Remember that the happiest people are not those getting more, but those giving more." When you start incorporating this mindset into your life, you will naturally begin giving out compliments, showing everyone respect, and helping those around you. When you do this, your kindness will be reciprocated. It may not come from the exact person, group, or source that you've helped, but eventually that kindness will come back to you just like a boomerang. That's because of the Law of Cause and Effect. This universal law states that every action has a corresponding reaction.

In other words, the choices we make (causes) lead to specific outcomes (effects).

When you help others by giving your time, effort, respect, or love without expecting anything back, it makes a big difference. Offering your love, help, or respect just because you want to means a lot more to people than if you're doing it because you feel it's your responsibility and you have to. By focusing on what you can give instead of what you can get, you will find that life becomes much easier and more rewarding.

# PRINCIPLE #15

## Love the Journey

---

*"The secret of happiness is not in doing what one likes, but in liking what one does."* —J.M. Barrie

---

It's a little profound that I chose the phrase *love the journey* for one of my principles, because I don't think anyone naturally loves the process of trying to achieve something. We love the idea of it, and we love the endgame—or the end result. But the steps in between from A - Z? Nobody usually likes doing those. Nobody likes the work.

That's why learning to love, or at least enjoy, the journey is so important. It keeps you on the path; it keeps you on your course and helps move you forward. It goes hand in hand with *Principle #8—Trust the Process.* When you learn to love the journey, it's much easier to trust the process it takes to get you there.

Here's an example from my own life: When I played football, I absolutely hated the process at first. Nobody sees the work you do from Sunday to Thursday. They only see you on Friday nights or Saturdays if you play in college, or Sundays if you're a professional. The grind in between the games? That's brutal. Early morning workouts, practice, classes, study halls—especially in college. It's easy to hate the process.

But the moment you make up your mind to learn to love the journey and process it takes to get you there, things get easier. For me, it was about finding the parts of the journey that I could actually enjoy, even through the tough times. I loved the camaraderie with my teammates. I loved being in the locker room, joking around and bonding. Well, in order to be in the locker room, I had to go to practice. In order to hang out with my teammates, I had to hit the gym and work out. I started to love those little moments within the process. I loved moments when I realized I'd improved on a certain technique. Well, in order to progress I had to embrace repetition. The small victories are what make it worth showing up every day.

I have a cousin named Rae Edwards. He's a former Olympian who competed in track and field, specializing in sprinting. Curious about his experiences, I started asking him questions about his training process and what it was like preparing for the Olympics.

One day, I asked him, "Is it all worth it?"

He looked at me and said, "What do you mean?"

I explained, "All that training you do is for just a few seconds of competition. For instance, in the Olympics, sprinters run the 100-meter dash in just about nine seconds. That's a lot of training for such a short performance, especially since the Olympics are only every four years."

He paused, reflecting on my words, and admitted, "You know, I never really thought about it like that. But I guess it would still be worth it if I were running for only four seconds every four years."

What I learned from our conversation is that Rae learned to love and enjoy his journey of being an athlete. He loved everything about track—his daily workouts, the camaraderie with his teammates, and even the excitement of traveling to different countries for smaller track meets. He thrived on the hustle of seeking sponsorships, knowing how difficult it was to secure funding in the world of track and field.

For Rae, the journey became the highlight. By the time the Olympics came around, it was the cherry on top of an already fulfilling experience. I'm glad he shared that insight with me because it beautifully illustrates the importance of loving the journey, not just the destination.

The whole journey is essential even though at times it might be tough and stressful. When I first started acting, at one point I was juggling five jobs, working constantly but not making much money. I wasn't getting any auditions because I was new, and nobody knew me. My joy came from attending acting class. Everything else faded into the background.

On Mondays, I knew I had acting class at 7:00 PM for three hours. That was my opportunity to do what I loved, and I could use my experiences from the previous week as motivation and emotional fuel for my scenes. That was my cheat code. I tell people all the time that I'm living my bonus life now. I've experienced life as a football player, something most people never get to do, and now I'm an actor, another thing most people never get to experience. For both of these lives, I could get my frustrations from the rest of the week out of me.

As a football player I could take out all of my emotions on the offensive lineman standing across from me on the field and then celebrated for doing a good job. Once I began my journey as an actor, I could take all my pain, frustrations, struggles, and emotions from the previous week and pour them into my craft. Going to acting class every Monday became the brightest point of my week. Being able to be among my peers, bettering myself in the craft, and expressing whatever I had bottled up was invaluable.

Once you identify those parts of the process that you love, it becomes easier to show up and do the work on a daily basis, even if the rewards feel postponed. Life often keeps the rewards just out of reach, so the more you find to fall in love with the journey, the better. I know I've done things that many people only dream of, and now I'm living another dream that most want but don't get to experience. I don't take that for granted.

When people ask me for advice about acting—and I get this all the time because of my background coming from a small place like Alabama—I often hear, "How did you do it? How did you make it coming from such a small place? What should I do?" My first question to them is always, "Why do you want to act?"

I ask this because acting is a job. I tell people all the time that it's a profession for ordinary individuals, but it comes with extraordinary suffering, responsibilities and sacrifices. If you're doing it for the wrong reasons, you'll likely start to resent both the craft and yourself.

When I ask people about their motivations, if their answers are along the lines of, "I think it would be cool," or "I thought it would pay a lot of money," then I know they're not genuinely passionate. If someone says, "I've always wanted to do this, but I was shy about how to get into it," or "I used to want to act as a child, but my mom said I couldn't," I can see they have the passion.

If they don't express that kind of enthusiasm, I tell them that they might want to talk to someone else or consider sticking with what they're currently doing because acting may not be for them. I know this sounds harsh, but sometimes brutal feedback is necessary to save people from wasting time and experiencing heartbreak.

Acting requires a significant investment of time with often little immediate reward. If you don't love it, you're going to find it very difficult. I advise anyone who is passionate about anything—no matter how little it pays—if you love it, you should pursue it. Because in the end, it will be worth it. You can make all the money in the world, but if you hate what you're doing, you'll be miserable. I know plenty of miserable millionaires, and the only reason they're unhappy is that they sacrificed who they were and what they love to chase something else.

Every day you wake up, you have to make that choice—whether or not you're going to show up. When you've made up your mind to find something you love about the journey, it becomes a lot easier. And really, all we can do is control today. Yesterday's gone, and tomorrow isn't here yet. So if you can focus on today, and find one or two things you enjoy about your journey—whatever it is you're working toward—it makes showing up every day worthwhile.

# PRINCIPLE #16
## Companionship

---

*"Friendship is a single soul dwelling in two bodies."* —Aristotle

---

Companionship is vital to human growth and fulfillment. As humans, we naturally desire connection. We crave having someone to share our lives, exploring the world alongside us, and building lasting memories together. Research by psychologist Dr. Susan Pinker, author of *The Village Effect*, highlights that social bonds are linked to long-term health and happiness, emphasizing that meaningful relationships are as critical as exercise or diet for longevity. There are two types of companionship that profoundly shape our lives: romantic and platonic.

Romantic companionship fulfills the innate human desire for emotional intimacy, providing a partner to share life's joys, challenges, and milestones. This bond is deeply rooted in mutual respect, love, and commitment. It offers a sense of belonging. Romantic companionships are most likely to offer emotional stability that helps us avoid the sting of loneliness when life gets difficult. This bond can allow us to create a family together and experience life more deeply by sharing it intimately with someone who not only supports our journey through life, but also enhances it.

On the other hand, platonic companionship thrives on shared interests, trust, and emotional support, free from the complexities of romance. When you're clicking on all those cylinders, and these bonds are nurtured, over time they can evolve into feeling as strong and reliable as family. These kinds of friendships are vital for personal growth and mental well-being. They can create a network of allies who enrich life in meaningful ways. Research by psychology journal, *Social and Personality Psychology Compass*, highlights how platonic friendships offer critical support during life's transitions, emphasizing their unique and lasting value.

I included the principle of companionship in this book not to explore the dynamics of romantic or platonic relationships, but to emphasize the power we have to intentionally choose who we build these connections with. This ability to select our companions can be life changing. The companions we choose—whether romantic partners or friends—shape the trajectory of our lives.

A foundational truth is that our closest relationships often mirror who we are. Motivational speaker Jim Rohn once said, *"You are the average of the five people you spend the most time with."* This profound insight underscores the importance of surrounding ourselves with individuals who inspire, challenge, and elevate us. Studies published in *PLOS One* (Public Library of Science) confirm that friendships and partnerships significantly influence our habits, attitudes, and overall satisfaction in life. This fact increases as we grow older.

I've been told by multiple mentors, and I've seen many interviews stating that the person you choose to spend your life with is one of—if not—the most important decisions you will ever make, and if you choose wisely there's no feeling quite like it. This involves choosing someone to stand with you during life's most challenging times. Choosing someone to build a future and family alongside you is not something to take lightly. I understand the magnitude of this decision, and I only want to make this decision once. I pray the decision for the future Mrs. McKissic lasts a lifetime. It affects not only us but also future generations. I look forward to building a long-lasting, deep and meaningful relationship someday.

A harmonious relationship brings balance to every family. A woman is not supposed to be behind a good man. Genesis 2:22 states, "Then the LORD God made a woman from the rib he had taken out of the man...." That means that in marriage you are in it equally. God took a rib from man because man and woman are to walk side by side throughout life. If a woman were supposed to be behind man, God would have taken her from our spine. If she were meant to be in front of a man, He would have taken her from our sternum. If she were made to be beneath us—she would've been taken from man's heel. If a woman were made to be above man, God would have taken her from the man's crown. God chose a rib to show she is meant to walk beside man—this is not a coincidence.

Companionship can be hell-filled and full of conflict or a source of immense joy and harmony. The quality of our relationships profoundly impacts our mental and emotional states. By choosing companions—both romantic and platonic—who align with our values and aspirations, we create a life that is richer, more meaningful, and more fulfilling. Research from *The Journal of Positive Psychology* highlights that quality connections directly correlate with increased happiness and decreased stress.

Together, romantic and platonic companionship illustrate the depth and diversity of human connection. Each plays a crucial role in fostering emotional fulfillment. At its core, companionship reflects our innate desire for connection—whether romantic or platonic. It is the foundation of human experience. Choose wisely. Nurture your bonds and ensure that companionship becomes a source of strength and joy throughout your life.

# PRINCIPLE #17
## Sacrifices Must Be Made

---

*"Discipline is choosing between what you want now and what you want most."* —Abraham Lincoln

---

Sacrifices must be made in every single phase of life. To grow, achieve, or obtain something, we often have to give up something in return. One of the most impactful sacrifices I've witnessed in my life came from my stepfather, Robert DuBose. He met my mom when I was two years old, and by the time I was three, they were married. Despite being a single man with a one-year-old daughter, he chose to marry my mom and embrace the responsibility of raising her two sons—neither of whom was his biological child.

Since my brother's biological father was still in his life, my stepfather didn't want to overstep his boundaries, so he never overstepped and made available to my brother what he offered me—the chance to call him "Dad," filling a void that existed during the first three years of my life. He willingly let go of the freedom he was enjoying to marry my mom and embrace the role of helping raise her two sons.

Although he and my mom divorced when I was eight, his sacrifice left a lasting impression on me. To this day, I hold tremendous respect for him, and still have a good relationship with him. His actions continue to influence how I view step-parents. Taking on the role of a parent to a child who isn't biologically yours is a profound act of selflessness, and I admire anyone willing to make that sacrifice.

Sacrifice is also very necessary when it comes to achieving goals. Sometimes we have to cut something out of our lives in order to add to it. This often involves giving up comfort, time, or financial resources. For example, pursuing higher education might mean reallocating funds from travel, leisure, cable TV, or other non-essential expenses to pay tuition. On my own journey, I've had to make significant sacrifices. In my early career, I juggled multiple jobs, working 17-18 hours per day, sacrificing sleep, time, and comfort to support my acting aspirations. I chose flexible jobs over a stable corporate career so I could attend auditions and filming opportunities and that meant less financial stability but more freedom to pursue my dreams.

Having more sleep, time, comfort, and possibly even money would have hindered my acting career, and I was not willing to let that happen. I knew that acting was something I wanted to do for the rest of my life. Sometimes one sacrifice can outweigh many others. I understood that in the beginning of my career there would be many sacrifices along the way that I would have to make.

Having a relationship was one of them. Being on call for auditions or bookings often meant leaving at a moment's notice, which didn't appeal to many potential partners. Sometimes I would fly from Atlanta to Los Angeles at the drop of a dime to audition, then fly back to Atlanta, only to be told I need to head to New York. No one wants a partner who is disappearing all the time and who doesn't have much time for you.

I've sacrificed a ton through the years—relationships, time with loved ones, and a stable routine. Now, as I advance in my career—as a producer, writer, and actor, I've gotten to a better place financially, but I'm based in Los Angeles. That means I've traded proximity to family in the Southeast for career opportunities. My family is thousands of miles away now. Visiting home requires financial planning and time management, but it's a trade-off I willingly make to build my future. Sacrifices don't ever really disappear, they just change.

When I chose my career path, I knew that at some point I would be living in L.A. That would mean when I wanted to visit my family, I would need money to buy a plane ticket, get a rental car, and many other unforeseen sacrifices would have to be made. To succeed, you must be clear about what you're willing to give up. If you're not prepared to make certain sacrifices, you need to ask yourself how badly you want to achieve your goal. Half-hearted commitment leads to frustration and unfulfilled dreams. Committing half-way to achieving a goal and avoiding the sacrifice usually doesn't make your dreams and the desires of your heart come true.

Being able to make sacrifices requires self-awareness. Knowing yourself helps you identify what needs to change in your life in order for you to achieve your goal. If you struggle with this, talk to someone who knows you well to help you identify what you may have to forfeit in order to have what you want. This is where it can get a little uncomfortable. For example, if you set your sights on running a marathon, you might need to sacrifice sweets or, if you hate running when it's hot, you may have to adjust your sleep schedule so you can run early in the morning. Understanding your habits and priorities makes it easier to embrace the sacrifices needed to succeed.

Ultimately, sacrifice is a choice. What you give up today can pave the way for a better tomorrow—but only if you're willing to commit fully. As the ancient Greek philosopher Socrates said, "Know thyself." Identify what things in your life may need sacrificing in order to accomplish the challenge before you.

# PRINCIPLE #18
## Be Comfortable Being Uncomfortable

*"Life begins at the end of your comfort zone."*
—Neale Donald Walsch

Many times, if you want to live out your dreams you have to get comfortable being uncomfortable. These two concepts are kind of related. They're at least first cousins, if not brother and sister. I say that because *getting* comfortable by being uncomfortable is key to achieving your dreams. To do that, you have to find something within the journey that you truly love. That's why I mention it again—when you're trying to achieve something, there will be a lot of uncomfortable moments.

I know an author who first started writing using a pizza box for her desk. The first thing I thought was, "Man, how uncomfortable that must have been?" Most people would stop right there. They get so used to things being comfortable, expecting everything to be perfect, or at least fitting society's standard of what a "stable" job should be. You know the type—those jobs that feel like security, where everything is kosher.

A lot of people found out during COVID that their jobs weren't as secure as they thought. Those who had *essential* jobs were fine, but many people who thought they had stability lost their jobs—either temporarily or for good. Before that, they would have said, "I've got a solid job." But the truth is, they were only comfortable. That's what I'm talking about—comfort and security. People get used to being in this rhythm of going to work every day and the predictability and sense of comfort that it brings. They get used to it because it's a familiar way of making a living. It's much easier than trying to do something all on your own. If you're working for a solid company, you know you're going to get paid and about how much that paycheck will be every week or so. That's a pretty comfortable feeling.

The moment someone steps outside that bubble to chase a dream, it's uncomfortable. It's not the usual path. Society teaches us a script: go to school, get a job, work until you're 65, and then retire. But when you go after your dream, it pulls you out of that predictable life, and that's when discomfort kicks in. People quit because discomfort feels wrong. It feels like they're failing, when really it's just part of the journey. They think, "I can't survive on $500 a week," or "I can't live like this," so they go back to what feels secure. What they don't realize is that the pain you feel today can turn into the strength you feel tomorrow.

You *can* do it. You might have to cut back on a lot of unnecessary things. The question is, how bad do you want it? How badly do you want to go on that mission trip to South Africa? Do you *really* want to be an actor? Can you picture yourself writing that book? Are you truly ready to chase that dream—no matter how crazy the rest of the world may say it is? If you really want it, being uncomfortable is beyond worth adapting to. You may have to cut back on some comfort, but if you love what you're doing, and if you're truly passionate, you'll adapt quickly. You'll make it work.

One year I survived on just $12,000. I was in Atlanta, Georgia, a grown man taking care of myself. I figured out a way to survive because I made up my mind that I was going to get comfortable with being uncomfortable. I made just enough to pay for my car note. I slept on a friend's couch, Jason Winston. I basically ate noodles, but sometimes I scored free protein bars from the gym. I pulled in a few favors from friends and loved ones. At the end of that year, when I went to do my taxes, I realized all I made was $12,000. I was amazed. It wasn't an easy year, but because I trusted the process and found something to love on the journey, I was comfortable being uncomfortable because I knew where I was headed. I made it work. I knew it was temporary, and I knew the discomfort was a sign I was moving in the right direction.

As an actor, there are countless moments when you have to embrace discomfort. Every set is a new challenge. Most roles I get, there are 499+ others who read for the same part. I don't feel uncomfortable on set because I've prepared for this. I feel that I'm meant to be there. I've put in the work, the "10,000 hours," as K. Anders Ericsson says. Ericsson was a Swedish psychologist who researched human performance. He also emphasized that it's not just the time you put in but in order to become a professional, you have to have structured and intentional practice. He states if you want to accomplish mastery you have to be comfortable taking constructive criticism. You have to put in that time and be willing to get a little uncomfortable at times. I've been a professional actor for almost 14 years, and I still take acting classes. I'm always training, always studying, always working on improving. So, when I step on set, I'm ready to go. Every sacrifice, late night, and hard-earned lesson along the way helps me carry the weight of my responsibility to deliver something meaningful whenever I'm called to do so.

I remember my first time feeling uncomfortable on stage. I was seven years old, doing my first play—a Black History program. They chose some students to represent figures like Rosa Parks, Malcolm X, and Jackie Robinson. Because we lived in Alabama, there were a lot of Alabama guys including Willie Mays and Hank Aaron. They picked me to be Dr. Martin Luther King, Jr. I already knew back then that I wanted to be an actor, and I felt like, here's my chance. The plan was for me to say just a couple of lines, but I lied and told my mom I had to do the *entire* "I Have a Dream" speech.

She believed me. The next day Mom took me to the library where we found his speech, copied it, and brought it home. Every day while she cooked dinner, she made me sit at the kitchen table and do my homework. After all the homework was finished, she had me go over Dr. Martin Luther King, Jr.'s speech. I learned the whole thing. But when the day of the play came—I was really uncomfortable.

I was really nervous and uncomfortable. I had lied to my mom. Soon she would find out that I knew I wasn't supposed to recite the whole speech. Everyone was going to have to listen to me recite this long speech because I wasn't backing down. I started the speech. I was about two or three lines in when I started seeing tears in the audience, there was a smile on my teacher's face, and I knew I wasn't going to get in trouble. That's when I knew I was meant to do this. Afterward, my teacher never said a word about me reciting the whole speech, I never said anything either. But I'm sure they all knew and laughed about it because I had pulled it off. They were probably amazed that I could remember that speech at such a young age.

I knew I was meant to be an actor. That moment cemented that dream in my mind. Even then, I had made up my mind to embrace discomfort. And that's a lesson I've carried with me ever since.

# PRINCIPLE #19
## Toe the Line Between Confidence and Cocky

*"The most beautiful thing you can wear is confidence."*
—Blake Lively

A confident person is someone who has self-assurance, believes in their abilities, and maintains a positive self-image. Studies show that confident people are more attractive and can inspire trust and reliability. Confident people tend to have better social skills and are more effective at communicating.

On the other side of the line is the cocky person. Cocky people tend to believe they are superior to others and may even look down at others believing their own personal abilities or achievements make them better. Cocky people may even disregard other people's feelings or contributions. They often brag about their skills or possessions. Cocky people can be charismatic but that usually fades over time.

There's a fine line between having confidence in yourself and being so confident that you appear cocky. I use "toe the line" here because it reflects the razor-thin balance between the two. It's also a play on the words "toe the line" in football: stay on this side of the white line, you're inbound; step over that line, and the play's dead—you're out of bounds.

When it comes to balancing confidence and cockiness, the same principle applies. If you're confident, it's typically because you're prepared, and you've earned the right to have that confidence. Most of the time, confidence is built over time through effort and commitment. As the English playwright, David Storey, tells us, "Self-confidence is the memory of success." Being confident is usually not an innate trait that we're born with, it's the outcome of hard work and perseverance. Practice and dedication lead to mastery and confidence in your own abilities.

People tend to feel comfortable when they sense true confidence in someone, because they feel like whatever this person is going to do, they will do it well. Like when I boarded a plane this morning, and the pilot gave me a confident, "Good morning." That simple look—his assured demeanor—put me at ease. I am trusting the pilot with my life at 28,000 feet in the air because he knows what he's doing. He's put in enough work to feel confident about flying the plane.

That certainty, that competence—it makes people feel safe, and most of the time, they don't even realize it's the confidence they trust and not the actual person. When a repairman shows up at your house to fix your AC in a confident way, discussing with you in a knowledgeable way what the problem could be, you trust that he knows what he's doing and will be able to fix the problem. However, if someone were to show up fumbling over their words you wouldn't be so sure that you had the right person for the job.

On the flip side, people can cross the line into cockiness for a couple of reasons. First, they've been doing something well for so long that they've stopped being challenged, and their confidence turns into arrogance. That's when they dip into the "cocky pot." We all know these people. They are very easy to identify. They come with a sort of energy that your subconscious immediately recognizes. It is completely overbearing, and most of the time we are not comfortable in their presence. It can be a bit awkward and annoying being around people like this for long periods of time. If someone in this category is challenged, they will either back down quickly and disappear, or over promise and underdeliver.

The second type of cockiness is just a mask. These people are not truly confident, so they puff up like a peacock to convince others—and themselves—that they're bigger and better than what they really are. They have not put in the work to truly feel confident, but they may brag about what they can do by saying things like: "I'm the best you'll ever see at …" or "I'm the baddest … on this planet." They may be trying more to convince themselves than you. It's all really just a show.

You may be extremely good at what you do, and that's wonderful. You've put in the work to get yourself to that level, but we all need to stay a little humble—no matter what it is you can do. The moment you feel yourself crossing that line between confidence and cocky, it's time to challenge yourself. Get out of your comfort zone, and shift or elevate whatever you're doing by trying something new. That's how you stay down-to-earth and humble. Now, I want to clarify, being humble doesn't mean minimizing yourself or downplaying your talents. Sometimes the statement "be humble" can be taken the wrong way or too far. Humility, in its true sense, is knowing your worth without making yourself smaller for others. There's also a fine line between humility as a virtue and humility as self-sabotage.

Pretending not to have the innate gifts that God gave you for the sake of being humble isn't serving anyone. It's certainly doing Him an injustice. Think about it: if you hide what you've been given in the name of humility, what are you really doing? You're not just selling yourself short; you're denying the world the very thing you were meant to share. God has given you those gifts and talents for a purpose. If someone feels inferior because of your gifts, that is something that is out of your control–it is within them and not you. You can't make anyone feel inferior. That's an inside job.

In *Principle #4* I shared how I used to slump over and walk with my head down because I was so tall. I was trying to take up as little space as possible so no one was inconvenienced by me. I am so grateful to my aunt for recognizing what I was doing and teaching me to walk with confidence. It was truly a pivotal and life-changing moment for me. I immediately felt more confident when I held my chin up and straightened my shoulders because I was embracing who I was instead of trying so hard to be someone else.

It's so easy to forget who you truly are, but my aunt wouldn't let me do that. And I'll never forget it. It's something that still crosses my mind today. I've never walked with my head down and my shoulders slumped since then. Confidence—true confidence—is attractive. It draws people in. No one wants to work with or be around someone who isn't sure of themselves. And it's not arrogance; it's about knowing your worth and walking in that truth.

When playing the game of life, you have to navigate the line between confidence and cockiness effectively. Recognizing your own strengths without boasting and remaining receptive to feedback is key. Challenge yourself to grow, making sure your confidence is grounded in reality and not inflated self-perception. Make sure to always appreciate other people's contributions in every circumstance. We are always building on what someone is doing or has done before us.

Avoid the pitfalls of cockiness by seeking constructive criticism and embracing challenges to refine your skills. This will inspire trust and admiration and create a ripple effect in those around you. This cultivates personal growth and resilience within yourself, creating a virtuous cycle: the more confident you become the more likely you are to take on new challenges and the more you grow.

# PRINCIPLE #20
## Get Your Seven Laughs

*"You've got to just keep living life and enjoying it. Don't take it too seriously, especially when you get older. Just keep laughing and enjoying the process."*
—Clint Eastwood

In one of his stand-up performances, Katt Williams said, "You know, you got to get your seven laughs." I've always been a fan of comedy, and I've always loved making people laugh. But more than that, I've always appreciated vulnerability. I'm not afraid to cry—something you've probably witnessed in some of the roles I've played—but I'm also not afraid to laugh. I've come to realize that a lot of the best jokes come from truth, and many of the funniest ones actually come from pain.

Laughing seems to help negate negative emotions. That's why I'm comfortable laughing at myself and cracking a few self-deprecating jokes from time to time. Doing this can relieve a little of the pressure I tend to put on myself if I've made a mistake or if I am struggling with something. Helen Mirren, who is one of the few performers to have achieved the "Triple Crown of Acting," winning an Academy Award, Tony Award, and Primetime Emmy Award, tells us, "Don't *be afraid of laughing at yourself. I think that's one of the biggest lessons I've learned over the years—take what you do seriously, but don't take yourself too seriously."*

Laughing can turn an overwhelming day into something that feels a little more manageable. Sometimes, making jokes about the challenges you are facing helps shift your focus from how bad and serious things seem, allowing you to take a step back and see the situation more objectively.

In March of 2024 The University of North Texas Health and Science Center put out a post titled *Why Laughter is the Best Medicine for Your Whole Health*. Stating that, "In today's fast-paced world, where stress and anxiety often dominate, the healing power of laughter shines brighter than ever."

Many other well-known universities and organizations have conducted studies on how laughter keeps us feeling younger and healthier. I've listed a few here to help you understand just how much laughter can impact your life:

1. Reduces Stress: In 2016 a study found that laughter significantly lowered stress in participants by lowering the levels of stress hormones.
2. Improves Immune Function: Laughter has been shown to boost the immune system by increasing the production of antibodies and activating T-cells, which help fight infections. Some research even shows that laughter can increase a type of white blood cell that combats cancer.
3. Improves Heart Health: Maryland Medical Center conducted a study and found that laughter improves the function of blood vessels and could increase blood flow by 20%. This is similar to the effect of moderate physical exercise.
4. Gives Pain Relief: According to a study published in the Proceedings of the Royal Society, laughing with others increased pain tolerance by up to 15%.
5. Has Mental Health Benefits: Laughing can trigger the release of serotonin, a chemical messenger in the brain associated with feelings of well-being and happiness.

6. <u>Improves Sleep</u>: Laughter helps relax the body and mind, making it easier to fall asleep.

Making sure you get in a few belly laughs throughout your day not only lifts your mood but also has many different physical and mental health benefits to promote your overall well-being.

I've learned that if you let the experiences of life get in control of you instead of you controlling them, you can go through entire days or weeks without laughing. Days that start sad, most likely will end sad if you don't step in and do something about it. Days that begin with stress, often stay that way all day long, unless you become intentional about laughing every day.

Whether it's watching a funny video on social media, listening to a comedy album on *iTunes,* or simply finding a way to laugh at my own past pain or recent experiences, I make sure to get my laughs in one way or another. I've drawn some of this inspiration about how important laughter is from my elders, people I greatly respect, and in several interviews I've seen on social media, I've heard elderly people when asked the question, "If you had any advice for young people, what would it be?" Their response is usually, "You've got to laugh. You've got to enjoy life."

When I first started embracing this philosophy about seven or eight years ago, it brought me immense joy. Hearing people in their 90s echo this sentiment makes me realize that making space for laughter can truly enrich my life.

Getting those seven laughs a day—and helping others around me do the same—makes even the toughest days easier to bear. Even when life throws curveballs or work becomes overwhelming, finding moments of joy and laughter lightens the load. And it's not just an emotional boost—as you can see from my little list, it's scientifically proven that laughter has health benefits. You can even burn more calories by being happy than by being sad, because if you're smiling more—you're probably moving more.

## GET YOUR SEVEN LAUGHS

I'm a big believer in getting your seven laughs a day. It's a practice that brings peace, energy, and a sense of balance to life. When they say laughter is the best medicine, it's no joke.

# PRINCIPLE #21

## Meditate

*"Quiet the mind, and the soul will speak."*
—Ma Jaya Sati Bhagavati

Meditation has been one of the most vital additions to my life, yet for most of my life, it was something that was completely foreign to me. I never even knew I needed it. I didn't grow up around it, because no one I knew ever talked about it. It just wasn't something I believed in. I can't remember when I was first introduced to it, but I started implementing it into my life around 2018 and began practicing it on a regular basis.

When I first started meditating, it was extremely difficult. I could only meditate for about 30 seconds before my mind started racing, thinking about everything I had to do that day or the challenges I was facing. It felt like a constant battle to stay focused. That's why we meditate though, right? To approach these challenges in a different way. Someone once said, "The goal of meditation isn't to control your thoughts, it's to stop letting them control you." I couldn't get anywhere on my own, so I began using guided meditation. This really helped me, but my limit was a total of about five minutes before my mind would drift, and I would lose focus.

Then I started a pattern and set a goal for five minutes each day. I would choose a guided meditation that I found online. After about six months, I noticed a change. One day, I completed the five-minute session, but I wasn't ready to stop. I felt like my spirit wanted me to keep going. I thought okay, there's something more I need to do.

So, the next day, I meditated for 10 minutes. In the meditation world—that's a big jump, but after it was over I felt great. For about a year, 10 minutes was my sweet spot, and that's when I realized I was growing because of practicing meditation.

I started thinking more on the specifics of what I wanted to accomplish with my guided meditation. So, I refined my meditation practice by focusing on specific themes like balance, prosperity, or manifestation. Some days I would decide that I wanted to focus on being prosperous, other days on being balanced—my choices were endless. I did all different ones throughout the week. This made the experience more conducive and aligned with my personal growth. Before that, the requirements for the meditations I chose only had to be within the time frame that I wanted.

Through meditation, I've discovered that many of the mental and physical limitations we place on ourselves can be overcome, and I've witnessed breakthroughs not just in myself, but in others too. Some things that I thought would be impossible manifested for me because of meditation. Meditation holds the keys for you wherever you want to go emotionally, spiritually, mentally, and physically. One of the most intelligent and profound people I know, a great friend of mine, Dr. Mikaelah Sarasvati PsyD, says all of this in such a beautiful way:

*"I like to think of meditation as the universal practice that the soul needs to boundlessly thrive from one level of enlightenment to the next. It strengthens the body's ability to perceive and create a more powerful existence in this dimension, as well as in parallel ones. Meditation is your secret weapon for activating the divine within you—the essence that resides in your temple—birthing untainted self-control, enhanced*

*spiritual attunement, and regulating the body's neural pathways in ways that terrestrial substances never will."*

Today, after six years of meditation, I no longer need to have a guided meditation. I can meditate in public spaces, even in chaotic environments like airports. I can't do it very long, but meditation has become a natural part of my routine, helping me center myself before tackling mentally demanding tasks. My advice for beginners? Don't focus on anyone else's experience. Start where you are. If you can only meditate for 30 seconds, that's fine—just begin. Find a quiet space, turn off your phone, and be present.

One thing that helped me when I was first starting out was finding a space where there are no interruptions, no noise or outside interference. When I closed my eyes, I would imagine myself in the most beautiful, peaceful space. For me, it was something I had actually seen. For a time, it was the screensaver on my laptop—an image of a serene prairie with a gorgeous mountain backdrop at dusk. I would close my eyes and picture myself sitting there, letting that wonderful image ground me. Over time, I added calming meditation music in the background, which made it even easier to focus.

Another technique that has worked for me, if mentally I have a lot going on and need to refocus, is imagining myself in a white space and looking at myself from above. It's like my soul is observing my body from a higher perspective. This helps me detach and center myself, allowing my soul to guide my meditation.

As people, we often forget how difficult things were when we first started, especially once we've mastered a skill. That's why it's important to remember the small steps we took to get over those initial hurdles. For me, going from 30 seconds to five minutes felt like winning the Super Bowl. And now, I'm able to meditate effortlessly in ways that once seemed impossible.

There are many people who have been meditating for years, but they can't really tell you how to begin. Anytime you are exploring something new, make a mental note on how you feel in that moment. Ask yourself these questions: *What am I struggling with? Why am I struggling?* Remember the things that were necessary to get you over that hump so that you may be able to help someone else with those very things that challenged you in the beginning.

There are some things that can't just be shown to you—they have to be broken down into little, easy steps so that someone just starting out can understand. Recently, I learned how to play chess. Dr. Sarasvati broke it down in a very simple and easy way for me to understand. For years I wanted to play, but until Dr. Sarasvati, no one could explain it in a way for me to understand.

To those who are new to meditation, or unsure where to begin, I suggest starting with a guided meditation or calming music. For those who struggle with a wandering mind, find your beautiful space, your place of serenity—whether it's a scene from a trip you've taken to a beach, a lake, or a mountain view—and sit there in your mind. Let yourself be immersed and embrace that moment of peace for as long as you can. If you can only meditate for 30 seconds, again, that's okay. Reward yourself, because it's more than you were doing before. This is your starting point. Even if you only add one second per week you'll eventually get to a time when it begins to make a difference.

Here is an encouraging statistic: *The Institute for Natural Medicine and Prevention* published a study in *The American Journal of Health Promotion* in 2011 citing that people who meditate regularly have a 43% reduction in the use of health services compared to non-meditators. That's incredible! Many studies since then have come to the same conclusion—meditation helps prevent disease. Rightfully so, the word 'disease,' when broken down, is simply dis-ease. When your body isn't at ease, sicknesses can form. So, meditation can literally be vital to your life.

I think a lot of people question things they don't understand. For me, it became clear, probably during college, that I had been closed off to many things because of religion—not spirituality. People sometimes tend to focus more on the religion of things rather than the relationship of things. I'd much rather have a stronger relationship with God than just a strong connection with my church. People can end up worshiping the church but miss out on building that relationship with God.

So, I decided to venture out and explore things on my own. The more I did, the more I appreciated certain aspects of other faiths. For instance, I came to respect the practice of praying every three hours, and I began spending more time with God than I had been. I also saw the value in meditation, something I hadn't prioritized before. I began thinking about how some of these new ideas were actually found in the scriptures I had been reading all of my life.

For example, this scripture from Matthew 14:13 says, "When the Messiah heard what had happened, He withdrew to a solitary place." Similarly, in Mark 1:35, "Very early in the morning, while it was still dark, the Messiah got up and went to a solitary place where He prayed."

Over the past year, I've come across teachings that dive deeper into scripture. One of the most profound moments was when a teacher broke down passages in ways I had never experienced. For example, the Hebrew translations revealed so much more depth about the Messiah's actions before choosing His disciples. He didn't just go to the mountains to pray; He spent entire nights there. It's said He went there to pray, but if He was there for eight hours, some of that time had to involve meditating, reflecting, and being alone with His thoughts. We weren't taught that, because many Bible passages are summaries—letters written from a person's perspective.

As Prophet Jones says, many of us engage in what he calls "appetizer prayers"—short, 30 second prayers in the morning and just before bed. But if you're only praying for less than a few minutes a day, mentally you aren't giving yourself the space to truly connect with God. It doesn't serve you or Him if you're not centering yourself. Longer periods of prayer and meditation allow you to become mentally and emotionally stable, which in turn makes it easier to hear God's voice.

Our brain can finally rest in a quiet and silenced environment. This is necessary for mental clarity and recovery. Resting in silence helps your brain recalibrate and improves its function.

Many people go through their day praying here and there, but with little or no results. It's because their minds are cluttered, and their emotions are all over the place. They can't hear God to fix the internal turmoil. Mental and emotional clarity go hand in hand with prayer and meditation. When we quiet our minds, we open ourselves to a deeper connection to our soul and ultimately to God.

Every day right after I wake up, the first two things I do are meditate and pray. Everything that follows usually falls into place because of it. So, if you're only praying without centering yourself through meditation, mentally and emotionally, you're missing out on so much.

# PRINCIPLE #22
## There's Only One You, Be You

> *"Your need for acceptance can make you invisible in this world. Don't let anything stand in the way of the light that shines through this form. Risk being seen in all of your glory."*
> — Jim Carrey

Growing up, I always wanted an identical twin brother. My mom often dressed my older brother Terrell and me alike, even though we were six years apart. So, you had a 12-year-old and a 6-year-old dressed in the same outfits, which I loved and I'm sure he hated. As a child, I would look at identical twins and imagine how cool it would be to have one—someone just like me. I thought about all the fun things we could do together.

My older brother was my first role model, and everywhere he went, I wanted to go. If he went outside, I wanted to go outside. If he went to the store, I wanted to go too. Even when he went to his father's house, I wanted to tag along. My mom would say, "No, you should stay here with me and let him spend time with his dad."

My brother's dad, Tyrone McKissic, is a wonderful man. When he found out I wanted to come along he started inviting me. He'd say, "It's okay. I look at you like a son too." So, on weekends, when Terrell went to visit, sometimes they'd let me go too, and for me, that was the best thing in the world.

But even with that bond, I still found myself envying the twins in my family. *We have a lot of twins in our family.* I would think, "Man, I wish I had a twin—someone who looks, talks, and acts just like me." As I got older, though, I realized that even identical twins are different. Their faces may look the same, but parents can always tell the difference, and after spending enough time around them, anyone can see it too.

I have a set of younger identical twin cousins, just three years younger than me. After about 12 years of being around them, I could finally tell them apart. I was surprised when I learned in college that even identical twins have different fingerprints. Everyone on Earth has a unique fingerprint. That fact spoke volumes to me because it made me realize that even identical twins are individuals. They have their own gifts, talents, and distinct personalities. Even though they come into this world together, one is always born first. Think about this: sometimes twins are born in two different years—one twin is born on New Year's Eve, and the other is born on New Year's Day. And even though they may enter the world close in time, they won't leave it together. We all have our own dates of birth, unique experiences, different paths to walk, and personal expiration date.

It's so important for each of us to embrace our own identities and unique personalities. We must all listen to the voice within that is directing us toward our individual calling. In a world full of leaders and followers, many people (especially young children) follow in the footsteps of others. For me, it was my older brother's footsteps. But the more I grew, the more I started becoming comfortable with who I was. I started venturing off into being Jock McKissic, and doing what I wanted to do, instead of making my decisions on what Terrell McKissic was doing.

It's important to point out that young children need to have good role models because they naturally look up to people who are older, stronger, or more experienced than they are. Instinct tells them to follow someone "bigger." It's part of how they learn about the world and develop their own behavior. Children are highly impressionable. They will often imitate what they see, especially from those they admire or trust. A positive role model can shape a child's values, teaching them about kindness and responsibility. According to *National Mentoring Partnership*, young people with a positive role model are 46% more likely to hold leadership positions.

Once you come to the realization that the gifts God gave you are unique to you, you understand how special you really are. Once we begin growing up—it's really all up to us to decide if we're going to spend our lives chasing someone else's dreams or creating our own. To me, unless you're a young child, following in someone else's footsteps or ignoring your own gifts is a waste of time. When you take pride in your name, trust God, and embrace who you really are, being YOU will come naturally.

# PRINCIPLE #23
## Flowers for the Living

*"There are high spots in all of our lives, and most of them have come about through encouragement from someone else."* —George M. Adams

This principle is one of my favorites, because of the simple and unique importance it holds. Not many people view the world this way. When people embrace this principle, it seems to make them better humans. By the time I was around 14 or 15, I started seeing the world from a very individual viewpoint. I'm not claiming to be perfect, but I think this is one of my most illustrious traits, maybe even a gift. I began noticing and questioning things that didn't make sense to me. I would ponder questions in my mind thinking, "Why is this?" or "Why are things that way?" One of my questions was, "Why do we often miss chances to truly appreciate people while they're alive?"

At this point in my life, I had attended a few family members' funerals where I heard people stand up to speak about the deceased, offering all of these beautiful and heartfelt stories about how wonderful they were. Yet, these words often came from people who were never around or rarely spent time with the person. Some who hadn't seen them for years would be in shambles, wishing they'd told the deceased how much they loved or appreciated them while they were still walking this earth, now they would never get that chance. I listened and observed. I decided that I didn't want to be one of those people who only shared kind words after it was too late. I wanted my loved ones to know how I felt about them while they were alive, so they'd never have to wonder.

For those who are truly closest to me, when they transition and leave me behind, I want them to go knowing I did all I could to support and uplift them. If they were lying on their deathbed and someone asked them, *"What's your relationship with Jock McKissic?"* I'd want them to say, *"I know he loves, respects, and cherishes me."* I began viewing relationships differently, realizing that I wanted to live in a way that left no room for regret or unexpressed appreciation.

Then there's the symbolism of flowers. In the United States it has been estimated that every year, anywhere from between $500 million and $1 billion dollars are spent on flowers for funerals. At most funerals, you'll see flowers everywhere—bouquets on top of the casket, arrangements from friends, family, old classmates, even just simple acquaintances. But the person inside the casket, who is transitioning, can't see or smell those flowers. Many people will pass from this earth never receiving one single bouquet in their whole lifetime, yet at their funeral, they're surrounded by more flowers than they could ever imagine. This is especially the case for men, because in our culture, flowers aren't typically given to men.

So, I made it my business to give flowers, in one form or another, to everyone that I come into contact with during my lifetime. It became important for me to show my appreciation to people whenever I could. Not necessarily just through flowers, but through kind and empowering words, too. For instance, whenever I see a veteran wearing a military hat, I thank them for their service—every single time. It's easy, just: "Hey, thank you for your service." Veterans all around our great country literally put their lives on the line, defending millions they'll never meet, and very often this service goes overlooked or unappreciated by those of us who are enjoying the freedom—maybe even taking it for granted.

Saying thank you to veterans is my way of giving a little back to them through inspirational "flowers" of gratitude.

I also find ways to compliment people, especially when I first meet them. There's always something admirable about everyone you meet, something worth acknowledging. It may be a talent, an accomplishment, or just a good quality. So many people go through life without ever hearing positive words from others, and they start believing that there's nothing valuable in them. My goal is to remind people of their worth whenever I can. I empower them through my words and through my actions. I give actual physical flowers whenever I can. I don't ever want anyone I know to first be gifted flowers on the day of their funeral.

When celebrities pass, we see an outpouring of love from people who often never showed any sign of admiration until that moment. I've seen it countless times, and I realize that we don't appreciate people enough while they're alive. That's why, with the actors, musicians, and figures I admire, I make an effort to share my appreciation openly and not wait until they're gone. I'll post about them, sharing short stories about their impact on me, and I use the hashtag #FlowersForTheLiving. Even the most successful people crave recognition.

I love plants and flowers and always have some in my room. They are so beautiful. Flowers, both physical and metaphorical, have become a meaningful way for me to express my love and admiration. Sometimes I even give flowers to my male friends. When I received my first bouquet, I cried because I knew how much it means when I give flowers. Society teaches us that flowers are "a woman thing," but there is an abundance of them at men's funerals. Why should the first time someone receives flowers be at their funeral? I try to uplift and encourage my male friends whenever I can because of something Chris Rock said that has stuck with me, "Only women, children, and dogs are loved unconditionally." Many times, a man is only loved based on the requirement that he provides something.

Men are rarely loved unconditionally. It's often the case that a man's worth is tied to his ability to provide or fulfill certain roles. This is how our society in general is structured. Many women will marry a man because he's a great provider and he treats them well. If he loses his job—the woman may consider leaving him. A man, on the other hand, will marry a woman just because he likes her, she's nice, or he thinks she's pretty. A man usually doesn't really care about what kind of a job the woman has, he just loves her unconditionally. It's the same way with children and pets. We love them only because they're ours or they're cute and innocent. They need not give us anything to receive our love.

So, I give flowers in all forms to everyone around me. I look for moments to show appreciation and encouragement, and I always make time to thank people. A lot of people do things simply because they care, not expecting anything in return, but knowing that you're appreciated is irreplaceable. I sometimes show my appreciation and respect for women by opening doors and pumping gas for them. When it comes to men, especially fathers and husbands, I make sure to give flowers of appreciation and gratitude. Most of the time, it's met with surprise. The men will say, "Oh man! Thank you. I never knew you felt that way" or "I don't get that much."

Because of our society, sometimes it's hard for men to receive. Through my own journey, I have realized that I also needed to learn how to receive. I realized that I don't have to give all the time; I'm worthy of receiving, too. Many times, when someone would thank or praise me for something, I would say something like, "No, it's fine" or "No big deal." During therapy I learned to open myself to receiving. Some people give, give, give and never allow themselves to receive. Any gift, including the gift of praise, is a circle that cannot be completed unless it is accepted. This insight has inspired me to remind others that they *are* deserving of love and appreciation, of flowers, and words of praise.

If more people took this principle of "giving flowers to the living" to heart, the world would be a better place. Let's all make a commitment to try a little harder at honoring, celebrating, and appreciating people while they're still with us. Let's remember that praise, gratitude, and recognition are most meaningful when given directly to those who inspire us. American poet Langston Hughes said, "I'd rather have roses on my table than diamonds on my neck." I'm sure most of us would agree with this statement—especially if those roses came from someone we love. Heartfelt gestures often mean more than material wealth and especially more than posthumous praise. Showing appreciation in real-time gives us a genuine connection to those we love and admire. It allows both the giver and receiver to experience a deeper bond.

Don't wait to give flowers and praise until it is too late. You don't want any "should have" moments after someone you love has passed. Celebrating people now strengthens emotional ties, builds confidence, and ensures that our words don't go unsaid. In Dale Carnegie's work, he emphasized the power of "sincere appreciation," which not only uplifts the recipient but creates a ripple effect, inspiring more positivity and connection among everyone in the entire world.

# PRINCIPLE #24
## Manage Your Expectations

*"We must rediscover the distinction between hope and expectation."* —Ivan Illich

Managing expectations is a principle I regularly remind myself of, as I do all the principles in this book, but this one is important for everyone. It's a skill that applies to every area of life—whether in personal pursuits, relationships, or interactions with our children, spouses, bosses, colleagues, and just about everything and everyone under the sun.

Setting realistic expectations is crucial for everyone in life. If our expectations are too high for someone who may not have the capacity to meet them, disappointment is inevitable for everyone involved. This applies especially to significant others. First of all, we need to keep in mind that we cannot control them, and if we don't clearly communicate our expectations, they'll have no way of knowing what we hope they will do for us. Misunderstandings often arise when we assume others understand our expectations without being told, like expecting someone to clean the house before they leave for work without ever discussing it. You have to relay your expectations.

The best approach is to clearly communicate your expectations and, in return, ask the other person to share what feels fair and doable for them. It has to be a two-way conversation. This helps you align your expectations with theirs, preventing unnecessary disappointment or frustration. Now you have a mutual understanding, and everyone knows what to expect.

Managing expectations, particularly with children, is extremely important. As adults, we've already been through every stage of life that they're just beginning to experience. We've probably already faced whatever it is they're going through. We know things that they haven't learned yet. This often leads us to expect that a child should understand after being told something once, but that's not realistic. We need to remember that they're still learning, and we need to be patient. They need room to make mistakes in order to learn the lessons we're trying to teach them, so they can incorporate those lessons into their lives or routine. Constantly reminding ourselves to manage our expectations for children allows us to be patient and supportive as they grow.

When children sense patience and genuine belief from adults, they often feel empowered to meet or even exceed our expectations. This is because positive reinforcement, along with encouragement and patience, fosters a growth mindset in children—a concept popularized by renowned American psychologist and professor, Carol Dweck. When adults convey their belief in a child's potential, the child often becomes more motivated and confident. Adding patience allows children the time they need to fully grasp the new skill or concept.

Mental, emotional, and physical expectations for ourselves are also important. We must always be accountable for managing our own selves. We have our bodies, our minds, our homes, our health, our careers—the list goes on and on. Let's say for example that you want to be more physically fit. You set a goal for yourself to lose 10 pounds in three months. You can manage your expectations by doing the work needed to make sure you will lose weight. Maybe you go to the gym or do some other physical activities. You plan your meals and make sure that there are only good and nutritious foods in your pantry and refrigerator.

You have to put in the work or at the end of three months your goal or expectation of losing 10 pounds won't happen. You won't get any new results if you're not changing your thinking and habits in some sort of way. This sets yourself up for failure—mentally, emotionally, and physically.

That can create a cycle or habit of thinking badly about yourself. Beating yourself up over previous mistakes and failures is not a way to meet or make new expectations for yourself. Healing from past experiences or learning from past mistakes often requires time, whether the blame was just on you or someone else that was involved. By expecting ourselves to "get over" things too quickly, we risk being too hard on ourselves. Practice patience with yourself and take some new positive steps. Talk with trusted people or attend a therapy session. This can help you meet your emotional needs and keep a healthier perspective on life. Again, you have to put in the work.

When setting expectations for our relationships—whether with co-workers, bosses, loved ones, children, or friends—we always have to hold ourselves accountable to meet those expectations. We need to ensure we're doing the things that will lead us to our goals and the results we expect.

If my goal is to be a better husband or boyfriend, I must actively work on the areas where I lack. If I struggle with communication, I can manage those expectations by writing down reminders for myself—things like, "Make sure you're asking this" or "Make sure you're saying that." If I don't, I risk failing those expectations I've set for myself, and the relationship could be in jeopardy.

If my goal is being a better parent, I have to remind myself that I might be too hard on my child or that I need to spend more time with them. Writing down these reminders can help clarify my goals, keep me reminded of them, and therefore keep me accountable. By sticking to these plans, I can manage my expectations and strive to live up to them.

## MANAGE YOUR EXPECTATIONS

Managing expectations really comes down to knowing yourself and understanding other people. If it's someone that I have a personal relationship with, I communicate what I expect from them, and I ask what they expect from me. That way, we can have a mutual relationship where we're both managing our own expectations. Author Brené Brown is attributed with the phrase "clear is kind, unclear is unkind." Clarity in communication regarding your needs and expectations is necessary for fostering healthy relationships, both personally and professionally. When we fail to be clear, we may inadvertently set ourselves and others up for disappointment.

Be clear for yourself too. Write down reminders: These are my expectations. This is what I need to do in order to get this expectation 100%. I don't like deadlines, I like reminders. If we don't meet deadlines, we may feel like we've failed. I have short-term goals and long-term goals. I don't make resolutions every year. By telling myself "It's January 1st, what are your resolutions? I'm going to do this in February, I'm going to do this by April." I don't do those anymore, because I feel that I am setting myself up for failure and expectations that may not line up with God's timetable.

So, what I do say is, "I would like to accomplish these things this year," or "I would like to get these things done." I don't put an exact date on it, and then I have to go from there in order to reach whatever expectation I put on myself or my career path. I have to start doing the work—whether that's physically writing something, studying, getting auditions, networking, meeting people—whatever it may entail. I have to make sure that I'm doing my part and checking off everything that it takes to reach those expectations, if it doesn't happen in a certain timetable, I don't really care. I allow myself grace in that space because I'm doing the work, and it's going to happen when it's supposed to happen.

Don't be so tough on yourself by setting strained expectations because then you set yourself up for failure. Your confidence dwindles, and you will lack the faith to keep going. It's just a trickle-down effect. If you're clear on your expectations, and then if you've done the work consistently—you're further off than you were when you started, guaranteed. But if you didn't meet this timeline you put on yourself, you might overlook all the progress you've made because you didn't reach the deadline. This can be detrimental.

Give yourself credit for all the ground that you've covered, all the things you've learned, all the things that you've accomplished up until this certain point. You've accomplished so much and gained so much more perspective. Manage those expectations and always take inventory of the things that you've grown from. This makes life much more fun and fulfilling.

# PRINCIPLE #25
## Mentorship is Crucial

---

*"A mentor is someone who allows you to see the hope inside yourself."* —Oprah Winfrey

---

When we are children, our parents and the people closest to us are vital mentors because they provide the foundation for our values, beliefs, and behaviors. Parents, and many times grandparents, have a unique role since they are the ones guiding us through all the beginning and formative experiences in our young lives. Good parents and grandparents are constantly offering insights that are both protective and empowering. Their guidance often shapes our understanding of the world around us. Their example will most likely have a major influence over our work ethic, decision-making, relationship skills, and much, much more.

Likewise, mentors from outside the family bring fresh perspectives, challenging us to grow in ways that may be a little different or somewhat of a stretch for us. Together, these mentors build a supportive network that teaches us how to relate to one another while preparing us to face real-world challenges with confidence and integrity.

I am so grateful to the many wonderful mentors who have helped shape my journey. Some of my most impactful mentors were my parents, grandparents, and later Prophet Michael Jones. I was also guided by a whole list of others who have been invaluable over the years: Uncle Greg Smith, Johnny Lee James III, Tony Avery, Demetriace 'Chee Chee' Jordan, Corey Bedell, Spence McCracken, Dabo Swinney, Marion Hobby, Chris Rumph, Jeff 'The Judge' Davis, Tony 'Rev' Eubanks, Delano Finch, Brock Lawrence, Carlo Hughley, Bishop Kenneth Carter, and Ricky Wilson. In acting, I have mentors like Greg Alan Williams, Dwayne Boyd, Mehcad Brooks, Clifton Powell Sr., Isiah Whitlock Jr., Bryan Cranston and most recently, the great Laurence Fishburne. Some of my mentors have passed away, but their wisdom and teachings still remain a part of me: Mario Mitchell, Terry Dallas, and J.C. Lockhart. Each mentor met me at a different stage in my life—whether it was middle school, high school, college, sports, or the transition to adulthood and professional acting. Each provided a specific kind of wisdom that I couldn't get from anyone else. Some of them may not have known it at the time, but they were giving me little lessons on how to live my day-to-day life.

Without my biological father, I understood early on that there were places in my life that were lacking and the knowledge that was missing from our household. I knew that I needed to look for good men to be an example for me. I placed a great weight on mentorship from others. My mother is very knowledgeable in a lot of different areas. I owe much of who I am today to her, but if I needed to know something about the sports I was playing or simply being a man, there was somewhat of a large gap for her to fill. She understood this and was the one who encouraged me to seek mentorship from my coaches or other men she trusted. She even taught me how to ask the right questions so I could get the answers I was seeking.

I was smart enough to take her advice and ask for help with those things where my mother, though very wise, may have lacked the information or life experience needed to guide me in the right direction. My coaches or possibly one of my peers' fathers were always there for me and usually had the answers I was seeking. When you don't have all the answers, helping a child connect with someone trusted, skilled or knowledgeable in that area is a true gift to them.

When a child expresses curiosity in certain areas, it is our duty to help them cultivate it, because God has placed that interest in their heart. They may have a unique and hidden gift or talent waiting to be developed. By pairing them with a trusted mentor, the child can begin accumulating the knowledge and experience needed to succeed in their field. Lady Bird Johnson said, "Children are likely to live up to what you believe of them." By encouraging children to have safe and wise mentors in what they're interested in, we show them that we believe in their potential. This builds confidence. They may stick with it for the rest of their lives, or it may only be for a short season, but both are gifts.

Providing mentorship for a child not only helps them explore an interest but also clarifies whether it's a true passion. With guidance, they can quickly determine if a particular path resonates with them, saving time and energy that might have been spent on trial and error. If they do genuinely connect with this pursuit, mentorship allows them to progress more quickly, developing skills and gaining experience. By the time they reach adulthood, they may already be well-practiced, having already accumulated the "10,000 hours" it takes to reach mastery, as Malcolm Gladwell famously described. A mentor's guidance protects them from unnecessary missteps and often heartbreak.

In my conversations with young people, I always emphasize the importance of mentorship and the need to seek it. A mentor's guidance spares us from learning everything the hard way. This saves us time, money, and emotional energy. Research published in *The Journal of Applied Psychology* supports this, showing that mentored individuals often experience greater career success, including higher salaries and quicker career advancement.

I now tell people who reach out to me for advice and mentorship that they only "owe" me the courtesy to pass along the knowledge I've shared, just as my mentors once did for me. I actually learned that exact lesson from one of my mentors, Laurence Fishburne, or 'The Dean,' as I call him.

On set one day, I asked, "How does one pay you back for all of your help?"

He said, "Just pass along what I've shared with you."

I replied, "You don't have to worry about that. I promise to give back and share everything you've taught me." I'll never take for granted that I've had the opportunity to build a relationship with someone I've admired and studied for years. One keen trait that Mr. Fishburne possesses is the ability to remain equanimous and empathetic while conversing with you. This allows one to feel comfortable in their ignorance and more willing to ask questions and inquire.

For many people, asking for help is challenging, but having great mentors in my life has taught me that it's essential to put your ego aside if you want to learn and grow. Not having good mentors in your life is like being lost without a GPS. If you're trying to figure it out all by yourself and refusing to ask for directions—you might end up going the wrong way altogether. Asking for help is sometimes a battle in one's mind, especially a man's. It's like you're exposing that you don't know something, and that's somewhat of a hit to your ego.

One day I called my mentor, Delano Finch, to ask for a favor. He readily agreed and said, "If I don't call you tomorrow, just call to remind me." I agreed, but when the next day came and he didn't call, I held off on following up, feeling that reaching out might make me a nuisance. Three days later, Delano called me, sounding irritated. When he asked why I hadn't called him back, I explained I didn't want to bother him since he was doing me a favor and was likely busy.

Delano's response surprised me: "Don't ever make that mistake again. If I tell you I'm going to do something, I'll do it. If I don't call, it's only because I'm tied up; you can charge it to my mind, not my heart, because my heart is in helping you." And then he said something that has stuck with me ever since: "Use me; just don't misuse me." Those words struck a nerve, reminding me that mentors are here to support us, and if they genuinely care, they want us to lean on them. I now tell my mentees the same thing, "Use me; just don't misuse me." His advice taught me to set aside my ego when asking for help, knowing that most mentors have our best interests at heart and are happy to be there for us.

In today's world, Google and online resources are helpful, but nothing can replace the guidance of someone who has lived it. Tony Robbins famously said, "Success leaves clues," meaning we can avoid unnecessary setbacks by following the example of those who've succeeded. Each mentor brings with them not just technical skills but life wisdom, and that wisdom is often the real gift of mentorship.

The things I've learned along the way from my mentors and coaches have easily transferred into everyday life. My coaches may not have known it, but they were not only teaching me to be a better athlete, but also a better human. Each mentor I've had has shared insights that go beyond skill, making a lasting impact on my life. Some taught me about resilience, others about humility, and still others about navigating the acting industry.

I've learned that the best actors pour their life experiences onto the screen. My mentors from the acting world have poured all they know into me. They all echo that if one lives a life worth living, you'll become a much better actor. This insight is something I keep with me, both on and off the screen, and I try to pass this wisdom along to those I now mentor. A life worth living is embracing experiences, valuing relationships, and embarking on new adventures that make you grow. All of us experience the world and ourselves in different ways, but we all have the same needs and feelings.

Each and every mentor has filled in pieces of the puzzle for me, shaping not just my professional path but also my growth as a person.

This mirrors the belief of John C. Maxwell, who wrote, "One of the greatest values of mentors is the ability to see ahead what others cannot see and to help them navigate a course to their destination." Mentorship is about being guided by those who have already walked the path, sparing us from stumbling through life alone. Mentors have made maps of where we want to go.

Mentorship is invaluable—but not necessarily mandatory for success. You may eventually find your way, but mentors are essential for a smoother, more efficient journey. While it's possible to figure things out on one's own, mentors provide insight and wisdom that saves time and prevents common pitfalls. As stated previously Google offers answers, but it can't replace the lived experiences of someone who has walked the path you aspire to follow. The knowledge and stories mentors share have a depth that only they can provide. Life has twists and turns that you simply have to experience to truly understand.

As I reflect on my own path, I am reminded that my mentors were not just individuals placed randomly in my life. I give God the credit for aligning me with people who were not only knowledgeable but also genuinely deserving of the title "mentor."

Having mentors who truly care gives you not only a set of skills but a new way of seeing the world, equipping you to face whatever life brings. It is through these mentors that I've come to see that when you have access to the right support and guidance, there's no limit to what you can achieve. As I often say, "With the right guidance you can do anything on earth."

# PRINCIPLE #26

## Embrace Criticism

---

*"Criticism may not be agreeable, but it is necessary."*
—Winston Churchill

---

Embracing constructive criticism is vital for your personal growth, but it's equally important to identify the critics. Constructive criticism comes from credible sources who care about you and genuinely want you to succeed. However, not everyone who offers criticism wants to help; some people simply enjoy critiquing without having any insight. They go around giving out free advice at any moment of the day to anyone and everyone on earth just because they love critiquing and being negative. It is wise to stay away from those kinds of sources. It's part of who they are that causes them to downgrade others.

Seek out feedback from those who understand your work, be it friends, mentors, colleagues, or co-workers with relevant experience. They have to have some sort of knowledge about what you're doing. That's the first requirement before you actually embrace the criticism. Otherwise, the advice is irrelevant. I call this "identifying the fruit on the tree," meaning look at their knowledge and resources before accepting their input. For example, if you're an actor, criticism from a peer in your field can be invaluable because they understand your goals and the challenges of your craft. Their criticism can greatly benefit you.

On the other hand, if my best friend is a mechanic and he's giving me advice about investing my money, I'm probably a fool if I accept his advice blindly without first finding out how he came to be so knowledgeable about making investments. If he says, "I've been following the stock market for years, and I've made a ton of money," his advice may be of value, but if he says, "I don't really invest; I just think it would be a good idea," I would be wise to find someone more informed in that area.

Choosing the right critics helps you avoid unnecessary negativity and ensures you're hearing from those genuinely interested in your success. Proverbs 27:5-6 has wonderful insight on this. It says, "Better is open criticism than hidden love. Well-meant are the wounds a friend inflicts, but deceitful are the kisses of an enemy." This means honest criticism from a friend, even if it is painful, is more valuable than insincere flattery from someone who doesn't really have your best interest in mind.

I don't get emotional when it comes to criticism. If it's kind and from a friend—it's because they love and care about me. I understand the fact that they may have information that I hadn't considered or a different perspective on something. After all, two minds are better than one. Their criticism can add to what I've already created. Whatever it is I'm working on, constructive criticism can make it even better.

For example, if a seasoned entrepreneur friend who works in social media marketing advises you to adjust your strategy by saying something like, "Hey, I really didn't like your post. You might try doing this next time," that's advice worth embracing. Rather than getting offended or responding defensively, ask them for specifics: "What should I tweak for my next post?" Constructive feedback can be a roadmap, leading you to valuable adjustments rather than wasted time and energy. Take your friend's advice and adjust your post. If you get mad or blow it off, you may miss an opportunity to grow your brand and social media platform.

Instead of using criticism to their advantage, some people fall into victim mode. I encourage people to ask their critics for specifics instead of feeling like they are being singled out or picked on. Say to your critics something like, "Okay, tell me what you didn't like" or "Tell me how I can change this so I can be better here on out." If someone expresses dislike for something you did, ask them to clarify what they didn't like and how you can improve.

Personally, I actually enjoy criticism from people I know don't have my best interests at heart. I use it as motivation. When "haters" critique my work, I see it as fuel for my drive. There's little that feels better than proving a naysayer to be wrong. If they doubt my potential, success is my greatest comeback.

The most effective cure for doubt is great and tangible results. When faced with skepticism and criticism instead of engaging in pointless debates, going back and forth, worrying, and giving more life to what they're saying, focus on delivering outcomes. Worrying and debating only causes their opinions and negativity to grow inside of you. Doing this could cause you to start internalizing their doubts and to believe what your enemies are saying.

Conversely, when faced with criticism from those who don't support you, use it as motivation by thinking to yourself, *Okay, so that's what you think. I'll prove to you what I can do.* Use their doubt to fuel your determination, push to prove them wrong. Ol' Blue Eyes himself, better known as Frank Sinatra, puts it very clearly, "The best revenge is massive success." Let their words go in one ear and out the other. If the criticism comes from an enemy or someone who is just being negative, it doesn't really matter anyway. Tell yourself, *You don't want me to succeed—I'm gonna succeed!* By focusing on results rather than reaction, you demonstrate your capabilities. Instead of absorbing their negativity, let it motivate you to rise higher, allowing your achievements to speak louder than any words.

We've talked about the two sides to criticism: one is meant to build you up and one to tear you down. But both can serve you 100% if used wisely. Embrace feedback from those who care about your growth and let criticism from naysayers fuel your drive to succeed. As the Bible says in Psalm 23:5, "God prepares a table before me in the presence of my enemies." This tells us that despite life's challenges or opposition from others, we can experience joy and peace because of God's presence and blessing. Embrace criticism and your inner strength and know that with dedication, you'll succeed—your results will speak for themselves.

# PRINCIPLE #27
## Identify the Fruit on the Tree

> *"Beware of false knowledge; it is more dangerous than ignorance."* —George Bernard Shaw

This chapter is going to build on the previous chapter's exploration of embracing criticism from credible sources, or how to understand and acquire the important skill of "identifying the fruit on the tree." Too often, we may hear someone talking, we read something, or we actually seek advice from someone and immediately begin incorporating those ideas into our lives without verifying and identifying the source. We may even start giving the advice we've received to others before actually knowing if it's good or bad.

Navjot Singh Sidhu, a former Indian cricket player known for his witty remarks says, "Beware of the naked man who offers you his shirt." When accepting advice, remember to evaluate both the expertise and the motivations of the source. Does the person have the "shirt"—the resources or experience—to give helpful advice, or are they offering you something they themselves don't have?

We hear insights from friends, family, or even casual acquaintances and we naturally assume they apply to everyone. But failing to assess the source can lead us down paths that don't serve us, clouding our judgment and distorting our goals. Recognizing the quality, credibility, and relevance of the advice we receive is a skill that requires both discernment and self-awareness. I learned this from my acting coach and mentor, Dwayne Boyd, who founded Premier Actors' Network (P.A.N.) in Decatur, Georgia. He taught me to always identify the fruit on the tree.

One day in acting class a student began saying, "My mother told me I should do this ... and that I shouldn't do that." The advice sounded helpful and insightful.

Then Dwayne asked a simple question, "What does your mom do?"

"Oh, she's a nurse," the student replied.

That is when Dwayne said, "What you have to do is identify the fruit on the tree."

I was really intrigued by his answer so I asked, "Can you elaborate on that?"

Then he asked another question. "Would you go to an apple tree if you were looking for a pineapple?" He continued by emphasizing the importance of seeking guidance from people with relevant expertise—identifying the fruit on the tree. You wouldn't go to a palm tree expecting to find an orange. If you did, you would be disappointed.

This idea of identifying the right "fruit" teaches us that it's essential to remove emotion from decision-making. We often feel obligated to heed advice from those close to us, even if it's outside their knowledge base. The truth is, expertise matters, and sometimes the most well-intentioned advice simply isn't the right fit. Trust the advice of those who have proven their worth.

Far too often, we go to people we know and ask them very specific questions about things they have no information on or expertise in. Other times, people volunteer their advice with the best intentions, wanting to help us. My mom never did this, but let me give you an example from my own life—what if my mom tried giving me advice about things like football? I should be respectful, because I know she has my best interest at heart by saying something like, "Okay, I'll consider it." Then use the crucial skill of identifying the fruit on the tree. This would be a situation where I'd ask myself, "Should I listen to my coach, or should I listen to my mom?"

I'd have to choose my coach, because my coach knows the game. He's played it. He's coached it. My mom, on the other hand, was just in the stands. When it comes to raising a family, being a missionary, or pouring into people, I'd go to my mom first, because I know that's where her expertise lies. I've seen her do it over and over again. My coach might not have the same skills in those areas, even though he's great with football.

A lot of people fail to identify the fruit on the tree because they're led by emotion. We often feel obligated to listen to people we care about just because they love us. Maybe you have a unique yarn business. Your family members love you and want to see you succeed, so they are constantly giving you advice. In reality, they don't know anything about your yarn business, so why would you take their advice? Because they love you? This is where we get confused.

What we really need to do is take emotion out of it when we're identifying the fruit on the tree. We have to look at what the person actually provides and ask, "Is this the fruit I need?" If it is, then I'll take those seeds they've given me, but if it's not, I'll wait for a better opportunity to use those seeds when the time is right. You can have the best seeds in the world—fresh, organic, elaborate seeds—but if you plant them at the wrong time, they won't grow. And if you plant them at the right time in the wrong soil, they still won't grow. Identifying the right fruit is key. You'll know when, where, and how to plant the seeds, and that's how things start to grow.

To put it simply: match the seeds you plant with the environment they need to grow. Expert advice is valuable, but if it's given at the wrong time or for the wrong situation, it won't yield results. Identifying the "fruit" of advice allows us to cultivate growth in the right areas of our lives. So, before incorporating someone's guidance, pause, assess, and ask yourself if this is truly the fruit you're seeking.

# PRINCIPLE #28
## Always Look to Add Value

*"To know even one life has breathed easier because you have lived, this is to have succeeded."*
—Ralph Waldo Emerson

My mom taught me this simple phrase: "Always leave it better than you found it." This principle extends way beyond just material things. Like a home or a borrowed item, it can be applied to relationships and experiences, too. My mother was extremely adamant about this way of living. She drilled this virtue into my brother and me. Now, as a grown man, I totally understand why.

If someone returns something of mine that they've borrowed in even better condition, I feel a sense of respect, knowing they valued my belongings. It doesn't matter if it's a book or a car, as Maya Angelou says, "People will forget what you said, people will forget what you did, but people will never forget how you made them feel." Leaving something better than you found it has a lasting impact—it shows respect and gratitude.

If I borrow a friend's car, I return it filled with gas and freshly washed, showing I appreciate their generosity. When staying in someone's home, I clean up and put everything back as I found it; I even wash the towels and sheets. But in relationships, it's even a bit more essential to contribute positively. Adding value to a relationship doesn't have to be a grand gesture; often, it's the small, considerate acts that leave the best lasting impression.

Imagine a scenario where a wealthy investor visits a small town and is interested in supporting local businesses. Naturally, many would rush to pitch their ideas and request funding, which is understandable. The investor may have 30 to 40 people pitching their business and not even one of them considering how they could add value to the wealthy man's life. However, the person who truly stands out might be the one who arrives simply to bring him lunch, ask if he needs any help while in town, or offer a small act of kindness without expecting anything in return. It's this selflessness that will leave a better and lasting impression. As Emerson taught us, "The only way to have a friend is to be one." The wealthy investor will most likely remember the kind and thoughtful business owner, who wasn't only looking to gain value, but wanted to add value as well.

There's no harm in seeking support from those willing to give it. Obviously, the investor came to allocate funds to local businesses, but even if you're asking for help, there's a way to do it that feels more like a partnership. Rather than only presenting what you need, you might think about and present what you can add: "Here's how my business can benefit your brand" or "my company can offer ways of supporting your company" or "I know of someone who can help you with your P.R." Think of ways you can add value and support the person in return as opposed to only taking what he is offering. This approach feels more like a partnership and transforms a simple transaction into a connection. Zig Ziglar once said, "You can have everything in life you want, if you will just help other people get what they want." By focusing on giving value, we're more likely to build genuine relationships and solid partnerships. This makes for a more even playing field for everyone involved.

In any community or setting, I show up ready to contribute and make a difference. For every gathering I attend, I have a goal of uplifting or assisting others in some way that will transform the experience for everyone involved. This approach ensures that, when I leave, I've somehow enriched the environment, even if it's just in a small way, and left it better than I found it. James Clear, author of *Atomic Habits* says, "The secret to leaving things better than you found them is to leave people better than you found them."

By finding ways to add value wherever we go, we create a foundation of mutual respect and reciprocity. Instead of just receiving from others, it's essential to look for opportunities to give back, helping to create a balanced and even exchange. When we bring value to every relationship or interaction—whether by showing appreciation, providing support, or enhancing the space around us—we leave a positive impact that others remember. This in turn is beneficial for you, because they will be more apt to help you in the future.

When we give value to others, people are more willing to reciprocate when we need it. As Ralph Waldo Emerson wisely put it, "It is one of the most beautiful compensations of this life that no man can sincerely try to help another without helping himself." This mindset of adding value—whether through actions, relationships, or the little things—creates a positive cycle that benefits everyone.

# PRINCIPLE #29
## Love Boldly

---

*"Dream big, love boldly."* —Terrence Tillerman

---

This principle is kudos to Terrence Tillerman, a character I played on the ABC hit show *Station 19*. It expresses the importance of showing love that is courageous, forgiving, and unconditional. Terrence's character demonstrates this with his family, from supporting a son who is coming to terms with his identity to guiding his daughter towards self-love and inner confidence. In a powerful scene, when Terrence is on the verge of death, he asks his wife to encourage their children to dream big and love without fear. He pleads with her to make sure that their children always love, support, and respect each other, and encourages her to remind them that they will get flak from the world, but should only find love from their family unit.

His message is clear: love is an enduring force, a foundation for resilience, and a refuge from the judgments and challenges of the world. Terrence's wisdom reflects the different forms of love in Greek philosophy:

Philautia, or self-love, is central to his advice for his daughter as he urges her to find self-worth from within rather than from external validation. He tells his wife, "It doesn't matter how many *likes* she gets from boys on Instagram. She has to love herself first." As philosopher Aristotle believed, "All friendly feelings for others are an extension of man's feelings for himself." When we love ourselves, we are better prepared to both give and receive love. If we don't love ourselves, we could see genuine acts of love as false and unmeaningful.

Agape, the highest form of love, is often associated with Divine, unconditional love. This form of love embodies the ultimate grace, compassion, and forgiveness. This is the kind of love that we are given from God. Dr. Martin Luther King, Jr. once described agape as "understanding, creative, redemptive goodwill for all men." In Terrence's advice, we see a call to rise above human flaws and extend grace to others the way our creator has done for us. No matter how we may mess up, God always forgives and loves us.

Eros represents passionate love, which, as Terrence implies, thrives on forgiveness and mutual growth. This reminds us that in romantic relationships, love is not just about passion but about steadfast commitment. According to C.S. Lewis, eros may start with intense feelings, but it is sustained by intentional acts of care and forgiveness. My mentor, Jeff Davis, tells me the reason he and his wife have been married for over 35 years is because they know how to forgive. They don't hold on to the mistakes that they have made—instead, they learn, grow, and move forward without lingering thoughts of disappointment.

Philia, or brotherly love, is essential to Terrence's message for his twin sons. He urges them to support each other through life's struggles, reminding us that friendship is about loyalty, patience, understanding, and forgiveness.

Terrence's speech, character and family have resonated with people all over the world. Whenever someone reposts this episode, it gets millions of *views*. The love that Terrence had and wanted for his family is what all of us want for one another. At the end of the day, it's all we wish to have, it doesn't matter what race, gender, color, or country we are from. We all long for that bold type of love.

Many times, the negative things that happen in our world are from a lack of love. When you question people about why they've committed these wrongful acts, most of the time it boils down to them saying, "I didn't feel loved" or "I didn't receive love" or "I wasn't appreciated." They didn't receive what Terrence Tillerman gave to his family.

In the end, Terrence's "love boldly" philosophy asks us to love in ways that are active and courageous. Bold love requires stepping beyond our comfort zones, embodying kindness, empathy, and self-acceptance. Loving boldly means embracing others wholeheartedly. Love grows through sacrifice and forgiveness. We are all continuously changing and growing. You and your loved ones are not the same today as you were yesterday, and you'll be different again tomorrow. People will never perform exactly how you want them to behave. People are not perfect; therefore, you have to be bold when it comes to loving.

# PRINCIPLE #30
## Have Lunch with the Loner

---

*"Every person you meet has a story to tell, a lesson to teach, and a dream to share."* —Robin S. Sharma

---

This principle begins with a story, an act of compassion in a high school cafeteria. One day I was walking through the lunchroom. I had pretty much a one track mind to go and sit at the same table I usually sat at everyday with a group of my peers. However, on this day I saw a kid sitting all by himself. I'd seen him sitting by himself many times before, but this time I really noticed him. Something stopped me. I felt compelled to go sit with him.

I went to his table and asked, "Hey, is anybody sitting here, can I sit down?"

He looked a little frazzled, kind of shocked that someone was going to sit with him. He said, "No, no one is sitting here. You can sit down."

Sometimes I would see him sitting with maybe two other people, but they would all be sitting at the opposite end of the table. They were loners too; no one spoke. I'm assuming they sat together, but apart, knowing that they wouldn't be bothered or picked on at his table.

So, I sat down and asked him his name. Soon we were engaging in a conversation. In the midst of our conversation, some of my peers from our table came and joined us. Then the conversation became a group discussion—and the loner was leading it. We were all interested in what he was saying. He was telling us about the things he'd done and the places he'd been hiking with his parents. At that time, I knew very little about the world outside of Opelika, Alabama. I was fascinated. We were all learning so much from him, and at the same time he was also learning new things about us.

Then before the end of lunch, I saw him as a new person. Someone that I'd never seen before. I'd seen him a couple of times here and there around the school, but very reserved and shy. During our conversation I watched him change into a totally different person, right in front of me. My interpretation of him totally changed, and his interpretation of me changed too.

The biggest takeaway from that day was how much his confidence was boosted during that short lunch chat. I was quite popular. I played football, not to mention that I'm six foot seven, and in the realm of high school these things are considered very important. The feeling of being accepted by someone considered "cool" allowed him, maybe for the first time at school, to truly be himself. From that day on, whenever we saw each other, we would always speak and talk a little. We didn't become best friends, but to this day we still write to each other on Facebook. Occasionally, he brings up what it meant to him that day I stopped to have lunch with him and how it changed his life. What he doesn't know is that it changed mine too.

There's an element of courage in defying social norms. High school is known for having unspoken rules about social circles. Breaking out of these quiet standards to sit with someone new can actually change lives. Studies on social connection by *Harvard's Office for Student Life* have shown that positive social interactions lead to improved mental health and resilience. Sharing a meal fosters an openness that can be transformative. Aesop tells us, "No act of kindness, no matter how small, is ever wasted."

Because of the impact from having lunch with my loner friend in high school, I continue to this day to sporadically have lunch with someone who looks alone or down. Because of *Principle #11—Remain Curious,* I am able to have genuine conversations and really get to know people just by one single discussion. Most people don't like eating alone. Research shows that people who regularly eat alone may experience feelings of loneliness, anxiety, and depression. Whenever possible, share a meal with the loner. When we share food and conversation it naturally boosts our mood and emotional state. You never know when this act of kindness could change your life or someone else's.

If you're someone who is shy and mostly eats alone, solo dining isn't entirely negative. It can provide moments for self-reflection, mindfulness, and even creativity if you approach it with a positive mindset. Finding a balance between solo and social meals, as well as creating a pleasant, engaging environment while eating alone, can help ease some of the potential downsides. Try calling loved ones during meals or eating in community spaces to help make eating alone feel less isolating.

I'll never forget that day in high school when I chose to sit with a loner. I changed his life, and he changed mine. Anytime you help someone, you later find out that you're simultaneously helping yourself. There's no right or wrong way to have lunch with someone you don't really know or strike up a conversation. It's simply an act of asking some questions about the other person, listening to the answers, holding space without judgment, and allowing yourself to emotionally connect and communicate with someone. It sends a subliminal message of, "You are not alone." Everyone is worthy of acknowledgement and connection.

# PRINCIPLE #31
## Stand for Something or Fall for Anything

*"When the whole world is silent, even one voice becomes powerful."* —Malala Yousafzai

The principle "Stand for Something or Fall for Anything" is often attributed to Alexander Hamilton from his quote, "Those who stand for nothing fall for anything." Since then, it has been echoed by many leaders and thinkers over time. This saying holds powerful wisdom emphasizing the importance of having strong personal values that anchor us, especially in a world that can often feel chaotic or misleading.

Standing for something means having and upholding your core beliefs, values, and moral standards without budging. It's about understanding what truly matters to you and staying rooted in those principles, regardless of external pressures or worldly temptations. Once you have this kind of clarity, it allows you to align your life with what truly matters to you. This makes it easier to filter out distractions and stay on a purposeful path.

When you lack a solid foundation of beliefs, it's easy to "fall for anything." You just kind of go along with what everybody else is saying or doing. You may just follow the crowd without questioning and get led astray. Before you know it, you can be on a tricky path that doesn't feel right to you, drifting into behaviors or following others' opinions simply because you lack your own guiding principles. Being rooted in your beliefs and checking your moral compass before blindly going along with the crowd is always a good idea. Studies on identity and purpose highlight that people who are clear on their values exhibit higher self-esteem and tend to lead more fulfilling lives. Those facts alone are a good reason to stand for something.

Having standards, values, and beliefs makes it easier for you to know what direction you want to go. Maybe it's something that you want to achieve. Maybe it's something worth fighting for. Sometimes it's identifying people or behaviors that need to be weeded out of your life, because they are hindering you from staying true to your core beliefs and goals.

Identifying what you stand for gives you a sense of pride. That knowledge drives and motivates you. Knowing what you stand for encourages you and gives you answers when you're questioning which path to take.

Knowing what you stand for also shapes how you interact with others, including those whose beliefs may be different from yours. Standing for something doesn't mean that those with other views are your enemies. That's simply not the case. We can all co-exist peacefully. In fact, embracing diversity in thought enriches our perspectives. Politics and religion can divide us and create tension only because people assume that their differences automatically equal opposition. Yet, as Gandhi wisely noted, "Our ability to reach unity in diversity will be the beauty and the test of our civilization."

I personally believe that God drives me and that we're all put here to help one another. That pushes me toward more altruistic and benevolent behaviors. We are all influenced by others' beliefs. What are yours? Your beliefs can impact the future, especially if you have children. The way we raise and influence children will definitely make an impact on many people throughout the world and have a lasting impact on our future. When it comes to my mother and children, I never budge on my values. Anything that goes against my moral standards—even if there is a paycheck attached to it is totally not worth it to me. There is no price on integrity.

In the world of acting, this often comes into play. If a role comes up for me that ethically goes against my beliefs, I will turn it down. People question me all the time why I've turned down certain roles. I explain that I am a firm believer in standing for certain things. If the role depicts bad people doing corrupt things, I refuse to do it, unless the character is held accountable for his actions at some point. Sometimes bad stories need to be told to teach good lessons; this always involves bad characters.

If I play one of these kinds of characters, I never take my role lightly, because after a while, if you're not careful, you can actually begin feeling differently inside. The bad tries attaching itself to your spirit, so I try finding the one thing in that character that humanizes them—the thing that caused them to get into that low vibrating place. It's usually caused by two things: they didn't have love, and they didn't have a solid foundation of values and moral standards. If one of the characters I'm playing doesn't match up with my morals and values, I pray a lot and sometimes go to therapy so that I can make sure to separate my acting role from my true self. I understand that by remaining rooted in my principles allows me to approach these roles responsibly and maintain a clear boundary between fiction and real life.

One personal example of standing by a belief is my decision never to drink alcohol. I've never even tasted it. This is a choice that came from what I experienced as a child. Growing up, I witnessed people in our community struggling because of drinking alcohol. I even had a family member who died from cirrhosis of the liver—caused by drinking too much alcohol. I saw how addiction could take a toll on not only the individual who was drinking, but also their loved ones. I made up my mind when I was 10 years old that I was never going to drink alcohol because I did not want to be a reflection of what I saw it doing to those that imbibed. This led me to set a personal boundary, deciding that alcohol would never be a part of my life.

That decision has never meant judging others who choose differently—it's simply a commitment I made for myself. I've witnessed many people throughout my life who could drink alcohol, and it didn't affect them or their behavior. I have many close friends and family members that have a responsible relationship with alcohol. They don't abuse it—and that's perfectly fine for them. They have different boundaries than me and we both accept each other's choices. For me drinking was just a risk I didn't want to take. Making clear values based on personal decisions and experiences protects us from making potentially harmful choices, it can enhance our self-discipline and give us confidence whenever we are navigating life.

At the core of knowing what you stand for is a sense of purpose. Viktor Frankl observed that, "Those who have a 'why' to live can bear almost any 'how.'" Finding our "why" involves identifying the principles that tug at our heartstrings. Attach to these beliefs emotionally because those are the things worth standing for. You'll naturally protect the things you love and care about the most. It's a little bit of an oxymoron: having boundaries can actually propel us forward when it comes to creating a life that is grounded and meaningful.

In the end, standing for something is a continuous journey of self-reflection, discernment, and courage. It requires us to revisit our principles and reaffirm our commitments in every stage of life. By choosing what you stand for—and standing firmly by it—you craft a life defined by purpose and clarity. Then you can begin paving a way that not only inspires others but honors the essence of who you are.

# PRINCIPLE #32
## Identify Your Why(s)

---

*"He who has a why to live for, can bear almost any how."*
—Victor Frankl

---

Identifying your "whys" is one of the most vital aspects of achieving anything in life. Whether it's being a good example, raising productive and respectful children, or striving for a Nobel Peace Prize, understanding your reasons can make all the difference. Your "whys" serve as motivation when challenges arise. They can consistently drive you in those moments when you may be tempted to get off course.

Not only is it important for keeping us on track for achieving our dreams, it's also important for our health. Did you know that having a why is so important that the *National Institute of Health* actually published an article stating that, "Possessing a high sense of purpose in life is associated with a reduced risk for all-cause mortality and cardiovascular events."

There are many reasons for this. One is that a strong sense of purpose can buffer against stress, which is a significant contributor to chronic illnesses, including heart disease. Purpose-driven individuals are often more resilient, because they have better ways of coping. Another reason is because people with a clear sense of purpose are more likely to engage in healthier behaviors and less likely to have harmful habits like smoking or excessive drinking.

One of the first "whys" I witnessed was my mother's. She worked hard at a job she didn't love because she had two young boys at home that she had to care for. I'm certain there were many days she didn't feel like getting up and going to work, but her "why" got her out of bed and up and going for the day. She knew she had to take care of us and that was all the motivation she needed.

Because of all the wonderful things my mom did for us, my own "whys" began with her. Early on, I decided that I wanted to do everything possible to succeed so she wouldn't have to struggle. My dream has always been to buy her her first home. She's never owned a house, and very soon, because I've stuck by my "why," I will purchase one for her.

As I grew older, my second "why" became God. I realized that everything I am and all the gifts I possess come from Him. To not use those gifts would be disobedient to God. If there's anyone I don't want to disappoint, it's Him. Whenever I feel discouraged, I remember that every dream and idea I've had was given to me because He believed I could bring it to fruition.

My third "why" is something I'm not directly associated with, but it's very important to me—it's about inspiring young boys and girls, especially those from backgrounds like mine, who didn't grow up wealthy or have examples of success in certain arenas, in their communities. These kids see their dreams in books, on TV, on social media, or in magazines, but rarely in real life. I want to be that example for them. Knowing that my story could one day inspire them keeps me grounded and motivated.

They're part of my reason for writing this book, doing interviews, and going on podcasts. I want to show them that if I can do it, so can they. Who knows, maybe someday I could actually meet several of them in person. When that day arrives, I want to be ready and be all I need to be in order to inspire that person to move forward with their own journey. My aim is to be a source of inspiration, showing others that even the most challenging dreams can happen with courage, and faith, even if everyone else says it's impossible. This keeps me focused.

Having multiple "whys" for the same purpose is very important because they provide layered motivation that can sustain you through different challenges. A primary "why," like family, can drive you on most days, but emotions or circumstances may occasionally weaken its influence. A spiritual "why," such as faith in God, can become challenging during moments of self-doubt or failure. A broader, external "why," like inspiring others who share your struggles, ensures you stay focused and committed, even when personal motivations falter. Together, these "whys" can form a balanced foundation that keeps you moving forward no matter how many obstacles you may face.

The "why" I described above is long term, but short-term "whys" are also important. For example, one of my short-term "whys" was making my brother and uncle proud by making my first quarterback sack. I'll never forget the first time they saw me make a tackle on the football field—their pride in that moment meant everything to me. It was a simple, immediate goal, but achieving it gave me the motivation to push harder. Once that "why" was fulfilled, it faded, and I knew I needed a new one to keep driving me forward.

Another short-term goal I had was that I wanted to be the first in my family to graduate from college, and I accomplished that. My goal wasn't just about my success; it was about breaking barriers and creating a new normal for others in my family to follow. My cousin, Angel, now has a master's degree and is considering a doctorate. She's going on and expanding on what I accomplished. Seeing that ripple effect is amazing, but once I achieved my goal, I had to find a new "why."

In my acting journey, I didn't start with wanting to be the best actor in the entire world. I started with small "whys" that kept me moving forward. At first, I prayed that God would give me one line. All I wanted was to land one line—just two words—so I could officially call myself a working actor. That would make me one of the happiest people on earth. When that happened, the dream expanded. My next "why" became booking a co-star role with one full scene, then booking a character with multiple scenes, and once I achieved that, I set my sights even higher. Each milestone, no matter how small it seemed at the time, gave me the confidence to aim for the next. These short-term "whys" acted like stepping stones, turning what once felt like a distant dream into a tangible reality.

Once you achieve a goal, the question naturally becomes, "What's next?" and "What will inspire me on the next part of the journey?" Smaller or what I like to call "micro whys" are valuable, but they only last for a limited time. Once those goals are accomplished, those "whys" lose their motivational power. That's why it is crucial to have large and small "whys."

The ultimate goal for me has always been to reach a level of success where I can give back to my mother in ways that truly honor her sacrifices, like building her dream house. That vision feels tangible now, and I see it happening in the next couple years. The idea of giving back to the person who gave you everything is deeply emotional, and it's something I hadn't fully appreciated until it was pointed out. You raise a child not expecting anything in return, simply wanting them to be happy and successful, and when the child grows up wanting to give back, it's a beautiful full circle.

For me, part of my happiness is tied to my mom's happiness—seeing her without stress, without the weight of work or worry. It's why I started a personal tradition: every year on my birthday, I give her something special. While most people celebrate themselves on their birthdays, I see it as a chance to thank my mom for the ultimate sacrifice she made to bring me into the world. From the decision to keep me, to enduring the physical and emotional toll of pregnancy and birth, to the countless sacrifices she made ensuring I was safe, healthy, and provided for—none of it was small, and none of it went unnoticed.

Every year on my birthday, I'm reminded that my life is a direct result of her love, her resilience, and her unwavering dedication. Giving her flowers on my birthday, quite literally and symbolically, is my way of saying, "Thank you." It's my way of recognizing her journey and celebrating the life she gave me. If anything, this tradition keeps me grounded, reminding me that success is about more than personal achievement, it's about lifting up the people who helped you get there.

Identifying your "whys," whether they are big or small, serves as a powerful reminder when you're traveling through the journey of life. Your big "whys" give you clarity in moments of uncertainty. They help you focus on what truly matters when distractions and challenges arise. They act sort of like a compass, pointing you toward your goals, even when the path feels difficult or unclear. These reasons fuel your motivation, remind you why you started in the first place, and why it's worth continuing.

On the other hand, small "whys" help you tackle immediate goals, breaking down challenges into manageable steps. They provide the motivation and momentum needed to keep moving forward. Together, these "whys" create a sense of purpose, allowing you to move into your future with determination. They may even transform obstacles into opportunities. Your "whys" not only drive you toward success but also help you find fulfillment in the process.

# PRINCIPLE #33
## Read Books That Are Foreign to Your Life

*"The only thing that you absolutely have to know is the location of the library."* —Albert Einstein

My love for books really started in 2014, so it's been exactly 10 years since I began reading, avidly. Before that, reading for school was always about getting assignments done, reading texts, writing papers, and doing research. The only two books I'd opened on numerous occasions were *The Holy Bible* and football playbooks. I'd always prefer to watch something instead of reading. But what actually got me into reading was acting. I was interested in learning about different acting techniques, so I started searching for books at the library in Atlanta, where I was living at the time.

The feeling I had walking into the library was foreign to me. It felt completely different from the library experiences I'd had before, which were always attached to work—like doing screen work or writing papers. But this time, I was doing research for something I loved. The moment I walked in, I felt a sense of fulfillment and excitement that I had never experienced in a library before. I remember thinking, "I've never felt like this in a place like this." I was anxious to get into the library and find the books I needed, instead of feeling like it was the most grueling task in the world.

I found the books and went home. I read some and then I told myself, "Okay, I'm going to try to read a whole book." I did it, and it wasn't so bad, so I decided that I would set a goal to read three books a year. I considered myself a slow reader—not slow in speed, just slow in completion. I tend to take my time. I often reread chapters if something stands out to me, and I'll go back to it to really digest the material. I also take notes and highlight key points. However, I quickly realized that these were library books, so I couldn't highlight them.

I stuck to my goal of three books a year for about two years. Then, I found myself wanting to read more, but I didn't have the time to sit down with a book as often as I wanted. That's when I was introduced to audiobooks. I started reading a hard copy while also listening to the audiobook version of another book, which made it easier to fit more reading into my day.

I started with books about acting and different techniques. Although these were about acting, they were foreign to me because they introduced new concepts and terms I'd never heard before. I even read Shakespeare, which we all know can be eloquent and wordy. It felt like a new world was opening up for me, revealing more about acting.

From there, I began reading biographies about people's lives—people I knew nothing about, from backgrounds different from my own. Reading became so intriguing. I started learning a lot about the world from these new perspectives. According to research by psychologists like Dan P. McAdams, reading autobiographies and biographies of diverse individuals can improve empathy and understanding by expanding our perspectives. Engaging with different lives broadens our worldview, fostering a deeper sense of connection with people outside our immediate circles. I like the way Toni Morrison, author of *The Bluest Eye*, puts it, "The function of freedom is to free someone else. That's what books can do, they allow you to see through the eyes of another person, someone you would never otherwise know."

My own view of the world has broadened tremendously because of the number of books I've read and the types of books I've explored. Like J.K. Rowling said, "I do believe something very magical can happen when you read a good book."

My dream for this book is to awaken that resting child-like imagination in everyone who reads it. I want every reader who picks up this book to encounter some principles that feel a bit foreign to them. For the principles that do feel foreign, I hope it unlocks your mind and imagination the way my own was unlocked when I came across new ideas and words in books. That, to me, is a true blessing.

These books broadened my horizons, challenged my assumptions, and inspired me to grow in ways I never imagined. If you'd like to embark on a similar journey, I invite you to explore these transformative titles and discover what they might awaken in you.

Books that were foreign to me:
- *A Curious Mind,* by Brian Grazer
- *Contagious,* by Jonah Berger
- *David and Goliath,* by Malcolm Gladwell
- *Targeted,* by Nadia Nicole
- The 48 Laws of Power, by Robert Greene
- The Change Agent, by Damon West
- *The Color of Law,* by Richard Rothstein
- *The Secret,* by Rhonda Byrne
- The Seven Spiritual Laws of Success, by Deepak Chopra M.D.
- The Spook Who Sat by the Door, by Sam Greenlee
- The Way of the Superior Man, by David Deida
- Their Eyes Were Watching God, by Zora Neale Hurston
- *Think and Grow Rich: A Black Choice,* by Dennis Kimbro and Napoleon Hill

A few biographies that I love:
- *A Life in Parts,* by Bryan Cranston
- Barry White: Love Unlimited, by Marc Eliot
- *Greenlights,* by Matthew McConaughey

## READ BOOKS THAT ARE FOREIGN TO YOUR LIFE

*Prince*, by Ronin Ro
The Autobiography of Malcolm X, by Malcolm X and Alex Haley
*Undisputed Truth*, by Mike Tyson and Larry Sloman
*Will*, by Will Smith and Mark Manson

These helpful books are more in my wheelhouse.
*Break and Run*, by Bobby Lee Hodge Jr.
*Greater Than the Game*, by Stevie Baggs Jr.
The Scholar AthELITE, by Rashard Hall
*This Week*, by Mac Wells
Transplant with a Plan, by Etta Tawo

# PRINCIPLE #34
## Therapy, Therapy, Therapy

*"It's up to you today to start making healthy choices. Not choices that are just healthy for your body, but healthy for your mind."* —Steve Maraboli

My exposure to therapy growing up was practically nonexistent. The only context I had for it came from television, where characters would lie on a couch and talk to someone they called a "shrink." The therapist would ask probing questions, and after a session, the character would leave. That was all I knew about therapy. It seemed distant and irrelevant, and I had no desire to pursue it.

This idea was further strengthened growing up in a community just 15 minutes from Tuskegee experiment, infamous for the Tuskegee Syphilis Study—a deeply unethical experiment where 600 Black men, mostly sharecroppers who had never been to a doctor, were promised free medical care to join the study. According to the *CDC* during the study, which began in 1932, participants were told they were being treated for "bad blood," a common term in the area for a number of different ailments. In reality, they were unknowingly injected with syphilis and left untreated.

Many died, and those who survived often suffered debilitating conditions—including insanity. Some unknowingly passed this horrific disease to their wives who, if untreated, then passed it onto their children during birth. This sad and appalling atrocity shaped the collective memory of our community and cast a long shadow of mistrust over anything involving doctors, let alone therapists.

This "survival" mentality not only shaped the views of anything related to modern medicine back in the 1930s and '40s, it continued through my generation and is still circulating today. For many Black men, especially my elders, going to a doctor—let alone a therapist—is unthinkable. They remember well how not long ago if a Black man admitted he had a problem mentally or said he needed to talk to someone, he was labeled crazy or a psychopath. This often led to his arrest or being institutionalized in a hospital or home.

As a result, mentioning therapy to elders was met with ridicule or warnings. They'd tell you, "Son, you're crazy for even mentioning that. Those people will have you arrested. You'll be deemed a psychopath." This stigma made expressing feelings seem like a weakness. Add to that, for men, there has always been the societal expectation to endure pain silently. We aren't supposed to talk about our issues; we just dealt with them in the quiet of our own mind.

Combine that cultural expectation with the experiences my elders had regarding mental and physical health—where seeking help often felt life-threatening. It made me want no part of therapy. So, what changed for me? In 2019 I attended a Black entrepreneurial event in Los Angeles where there were young Black entrepreneurs from all over the country. I met a Black therapist. Initially, he didn't introduce himself as a therapist—we were simply having a conversation. He asked me about my life, my career, and my family.

Finally, I asked him, "What do you do for a living?"

He answered, "I'm a therapist."

"Like a physical therapist?" I had never met a young Black "shrink" so I was guessing.

He surprised me with his answer, "No, I'm a psychotherapist."

I had gotten to a place where I felt comfortable with him, so I said, "Okay. Cool." Then I immediately grew wary, wondering if he would judge me or start analyzing my words, so I turned it quickly and started asking him questions. He was so vulnerable with me about his life and his struggles that it made me want to have another conversation with him. I said, "Man, this is so dope, you told me all of this."

"Yeah, so here's my number. We should hang out sometime. Come down to my high rise in Long Beach. We'll go down to the bar or restaurant and chat."

"Cool" … that's how I got my first therapy session. We had dinner and it turned into a session. It was so organic that it didn't seem like a therapy session at all.

Then when we finished, he said, "This is how I have sessions with my clients. I don't do the traditional 'sit down in my office or lay on the couch.'" (My vision of what therapy was.) "I try to stay away from that because it typically makes people nervous or anxious."

That first encounter broke down my preconceptions about therapy. He became my therapist, and I met him several more times. To have someone give you free sessions until you get to the point where he can actually help is incredible. This man wants to inspire as many young Black men as he can to go to therapy. Everyone has stuff in their past, but the Tuskegee experiment, among many other hardships, is sown into the DNA of many young Black men like me.

I started realizing just how much generational trauma I carried, simply from having conversations and reflecting on the things my family, community, or people did. A lot of those behaviors stem from a sense of fear or tradition—things they had to do to protect themselves in the past: slavery, racism, societal oppression, etc. But now, as we grow and find more space and freedom, we're starting to recognize that some of those patterns are no longer serving us. I never would have understood this if I hadn't started going to therapy.

## THERAPY, THERAPY, THERAPY

Since then, I've worked with three different therapists and now attend therapy twice a month. Even when I feel mentally strong, I still go. Sometimes, it's just a conversation that leaves me feeling lighter. Other times, my therapist asks questions that unearth deeply buried issues I wasn't aware of. For example, when my therapist asks, "How do you feel about that?" I often don't have an immediate answer. He'll say, "That's your homework. I'll see you in two weeks." Over the following weeks, as I reflect, I uncover emotions and memories that had quietly shaped my behavior.

My family owns somewhere around 500 acres of land—300 acres here, 200 acres there. It's a legacy that was earned, not given, to my great-great grandfather, Mr. Thomas Jefferson Moore. Not a single acre has ever been sold. Generations of my family and my great-great grandfather's descendants still live on this land. Growing up with that knowledge gave me a deep sense of pride. Even without knowing all the details of what he endured, the few things I do know fill me with respect. For instance, the first man he worked for came and burned a cross on his land, destroying an entire year's worth of crops. It was all an attempt to sabotage his progress out of jealousy. I can only imagine what it took to recover from that, to keep going without letting hate consume him.

That kind of trauma, however, doesn't just disappear—it gets passed down through generations, embedded in our DNA. I often say that going to therapy and working to heal mentally is like literally re-coding my DNA. When I have children, they'll inherit a different set of memories and a healthier emotional foundation than my ancestors passed down to me. That's why therapy is so important—it helps us uncover the unseen wounds we carry, heal them, and change the trajectory of our lives. It's not just about rewriting our own stories but also shaping a better future for our children and anyone else we impact.

That's why I say, *therapy, therapy, therapy*. It has to be said three times because it's just that important. By addressing inherited wounds and baggage gained through living in therapy, I'm breaking cycles and paving a healthier path for my children and all future generations. "Trauma is not what happens to us, but what we hold inside in the absence of an empathetic witness," says Dr. Gabor Maté, an addiction and trauma specialist. Therapy provides that empathetic witness, allowing us to process and heal. No matter how healthy you think you are—you might want to give it a try. Who knows how much farther you and future generations will get in life by doing so?

# PRINCIPLE #35
## Representation Matters

*"The world is more complicated than it used to be. But I think that it is more inclusive, and it's important for us to build on that, to fight for representation and equity."* —President Barack Obama

Representation became important to me when I started having success in high school sports. I'd go out into the community, and younger kids would ask for my autograph or want to take pictures with me. I thank God for the mindset I had back then—the realization that what I do matters. That understanding pushed me to do whatever I was doing to the best of my ability.

When I went to college, I had the chance to do community service. I visited foster homes and met many kids, especially young Black kids from impoverished areas. These were kids whose parents had left them or who were in tough situations. They would talk to me, and as we connected, they'd learn about my story. I told them I came from a single-parent home, a small, unheard-of town, and an impoverished community. Yet, there I was at their dream school, doing what they hoped to do. Something clicked for them in those moments. Their dreams suddenly felt real—and achievable. They could relate to someone like me.

Sometimes, it's just as simple as having a visual. For example, like a woman running for president. Up until the first woman ran for president, girls didn't have any visual representation of what that would be like. When little girls see a woman running for president, they think—*I can do this, too.* In 2024 we had a Black woman running for president, little girls of color saw her and thought, *That could be me. I can run for president.* That's the power of representation.

After my football career, I took representation to the next level. For athletes, transitioning to a "normal" job after playing professionally or collegiately is one of the hardest adjustments, in my opinion, second only to what military veterans face. Many athletes don't have a plan beyond their sport because they've focused on one dream their whole lives. Most of them have been groomed and taught how to do one main thing—play sports. This consists of putting your personal life aside and doing exactly what the coaches tell you to do. You give up weekends and most of your free time for practicing and games. Then all of a sudden, just like that—it's over. Even if you have a great 10-year career, by 31, you still have the rest of your life to figure out.

I knew I wanted to be an actor next. I also knew the odds were stacked against me. I understood the fact that walking into audition rooms meant facing producers and directors who might've been bullied by athletes in school. They'd likely have preconceived ideas about me, assuming I was just a dumb jock. Ironically, my name is Jock, so I made it my mission to redefine that stereotype. I knew I had the choice and ability to transition from being captain of my team and tackling my opponents to tackling whatever Hollywood would throw at me. I was determined to succeed, knowing that if I did, I could open doors for other athletes who shared the same dream.

When I became the first former athlete from Clemson University to transition into acting, I didn't just open doors for myself; I opened doors for others. Now, there are four of us pursuing acting because they saw me do it and reached out for guidance. They were able to ask me questions and get advice from someone, like themselves, who understood exactly what it would take for them to achieve their goal of becoming an actor. For my younger cousins, seeing me on TV has normalized the idea that they can do it too. To them, anything is possible because they've seen me achieve it.

Representation matters because, most of the time, people need to see it to believe it is possible. If, while growing up in Alabama, I would have seen someone like me in my community doing what I wanted to do, who knows how much sooner I would've embarked on this journey? When you see someone breaking barriers, it changes what you believe is possible.

In 1954, Roger Bannister broke an historic boundary. He was able to do something that scientists, coaches, and other athletes viewed as an impossible feat for the human body to achieve. He ran a mile in under four minutes. Until he broke through that belief, it was thought that it could be physically harmful or even fatal to push oneself to run faster than four minutes per mile.

Bannister's success was not just a physical triumph but also a psychological breakthrough. His record-breaking run proved that mental barriers can be just as significant as physical ones. Within weeks of Bannister breaking that boundary, other runners began breaking through the four-minute barrier, further demonstrating that the "impossible" had become achievable because of having representation that it could be done.

Sometimes we have to break through barriers that others have put in place for us. Early in his career, Bryan Cranston did a short film with a friend, where he played a character similar to Walter White. Years later, when the producers of *Breaking Bad* were casting, one executive suggested Cranston for the role. Others laughed, seeing him only as the comedic actor from *Malcolm in the Middle*. But that producer insisted, based on the work Cranston had done years ago. Eventually, they brought him in for an audition. He crushed it. Even though he represented himself perfectly, they kept looking for two more weeks, but no one else fit the role. Finally, they cast him, and the rest is history.

In the acting industry, it's all about "show and prove." Often, people can't see what you're capable of until you show them. That's why your reputation and the way you represent yourself matters—it's the impression you leave on someone that could open doors years down the line. In the acting industry, and every other business, everyone wants to work with people who are talented, but more importantly, with people they like. When God gives you the opportunity to combine talent with being a great human being, you can't lose—it's just a matter of time.

Representation becomes even more powerful when others look up to you as proof that their own aspirations are achievable. That's why it's important to keep striving to do your best and to be proud of what you are continuing to achieve. For me, being part of a great show like *Your Honor* is another important layer of my journey. It's incredible to know that when people ask if they should watch it, I can confidently say, "Yes, it's amazing—you'll love it." The show's quality stands on its own, and I'm proud to be part of it. I would love the show even if I wasn't in it.

Representation holds immense value, especially when the decisions that shape your life are often made without your presence. Younger generations might think opportunities come solely from their own efforts, and while that's true to an extent, the biggest decisions—those that open doors or set trajectories—are often influenced by impressions you've left on others long ago. Your reputation, your character, and how you've treated people can have far-reaching impacts. It's worth more than gold, serving as a reminder that the way you represent yourself today can shape opportunities for tomorrow.

# PRINCIPLE #36
## Respect the Clock

*"Procrastination is the arrogant assumption that God will give us another opportunity tomorrow to do what He intended for us to do today."* —Bishop Rosie O'Neal

This quote resonates deeply because it ties into one of the most popular sayings in the world: *Life is short.* We hear it throughout our lives, yet many of us still procrastinate on nearly everything we can delay. I once heard a public speaker—not a motivational speaker, but someone who worked in Corporate America—share an impactful story. He explained that during his time in HR, he conducted interviews where he'd ask candidates a simple question: *"Hey, what time is it?"* He didn't ask this for practical reasons but to observe their response.

Some candidates would admit they didn't know, citing they weren't wearing a watch (this was before cell phones). Others would immediately check their wristwatch and give an accurate answer, "Oh, it's 10:30," or whatever the correct time happened to be. This seemingly trivial question became his tiebreaker when deciding between equally qualified candidates. The logic? A person who is attentive and aware of time is more likely to be punctual and disciplined, qualities essential in any role.

This idea stuck with me, and I incorporated it into my own life—not just knowing the time but being conscious of how I'm using my time.

# RESPECT THE CLOCK

At one point, I lived in a townhome with a shortage in the wiring system. Every time I used the microwave and stove simultaneously, the circuit would trip and shut off the electricity in that area. I would have to go to the breaker box and flip the breaker. Then I would go back into the kitchen and both clocks on the microwave and stove would be flashing. So, each time I would have to reset the clocks; I did it automatically. Over the years, I must have reset those clocks over 200 times, but I did it every single time without fail because I was very serious about knowing what time it was and being aware of how I spent it.

One of the most beneficial concepts I've learned is breaking up your day into "eights." Each day has 24 hours, broken into three parts:

- 8 hours for work
- 8 hours for sleep
- 8 hours for self-improvement, relaxation, or personal pursuits

It's up to you to figure out how you spend the third segment. It may be divided into a few different parts. For instance, four hours of *your* time may be before work and then four more hours after work. Whatever it is, you have to figure out how you're going to spend those eight hours. To aspiring entrepreneurs, artists, or anyone with a dream, those eight hours outside of work and sleep are crucial. Whether it's early in the morning or late at night, this is the time to invest in your craft, develop skills and/or strategize for your future.

However, balance is key. As mentioned in *Principle #5—Structure Your Day*, it's not just about squeezing more into your day. It's also important to make sure you have the energy to enjoy it. Taking care of your mental health is essential. You can do this by engaging in activities that you enjoy. Make sure to do something every day that refreshes and rejuvenates your mind, body, and soul. Don't squander those precious hours on things that don't add value to your health, goals, or dreams.

Be attentive to the clock. The last thing you want to do is work eight hours, sleep for 12 and then use up four hours by not doing something that is beneficial to your life, health, or dreams. In doing so, you will have wasted eight whole hours, 480 minutes, 28,800 seconds. That's a lot of time.

I don't subscribe to the mantra *"Sleep when you're dead."* Rest is not optional—it's essential. According to the *Sleep Foundation,* sleep supports brain plasticity, which is essential for memory consolidation and cognitive skills. During sleep, the body also repairs tissues, grows muscles, synthesizes proteins, promotes a healthy immune system , lowers blood pressure, and helps maintain balanced insulin levels, among other important functions.

I haven't always gotten my rest. When I was younger, there were times in my life where I worked so many hours at several different jobs that I was only getting about four or five hours of sleep per day. Now that I know how important sleep actually is, I don't do that anymore; it's just not sustainable. Everyone needs rest. For me seven to eight hours is perfect.

That said, respecting the clock is paramount. It's smart and beneficial to be aware of how you're spending your time. We all have a start date and an expiration date, yet none of us know when the latter will come. The time we have is limited, and every day is an opportunity to use it wisely.

Time is precious for sure. We have to respect the clock and be sure we're getting as much done as possible for ourselves and others on a daily basis. William Penn once said, "Time is what we want most but use worst." There are many different things you can accomplish within only five minutes time:

1. Perform a quick workout: do a few burpees, some push-ups, or even a little yoga.

2. Declutter a small area like your desk, a drawer, or your email inbox.
3. Send a thoughtful text or voice note to a friend or family member. A quick check-in can strengthen relationships.
4. Read a few pages of a book or listen to an inspiring podcast snippet.
5. Review your to-do list to align your priorities for the day.
6. Briefly practice mindfulness or meditation.
7. Get your house in order: (Folding a load of laundry, washing a sink full of dishes, or making your bed only takes a few minutes.)
8. Jot down ideas for a project, draw, sketch, or brainstorm solutions to a challenge.
9. Meal prep: chop vegetables, marinate ingredients, or prepare a small snack.
10. Write a list of 10 things you're grateful for. (This can help if you're feeling down or stuck.)

In only five quick minutes, you can accomplish more than you might expect. As the Greek philosopher Seneca said, "It is not that we have a short time to live, but that we waste much of it." Being intentional with our time allows us to live fully. It's not just about making the most of today, but also about embracing each moment with gratitude for the opportunity it presents.

# PRINCIPLE #37
## Proverbs 27:17

*"As iron sharpens iron, so one person sharpens another."*
—Proverbs 27:17

"Just as iron sharpens iron, so one man might sharpen another." This is probably my favorite Bible verse, simply because people often forget how important it is to consider how we're treating one another on this earth. People read the Bible for help or promises from God but tend to forget that we must not only govern ourselves, but we must also be held accountable for each other as well. Proverbs 27:17 stands out—reminding us that we must hold each other accountable and also help one another. It's become one of my mottos over the years. Whatever knowledge I've been given, it's my duty—and my pleasure—to share it with my fellow man or woman. If there's a way I can help someone without putting myself in harm's way, this verse always reminds me to do just that.

You see this often in the workout culture, where people have accountability partners. If someone slacks off during a workout or diet, their partner steps in to hold them accountable. That's an example of iron sharpening iron—making each other better.

On the flip side, people often talk about the "crabs in a barrel" mentality, where others pull each other down so no one gets ahead of those on the bottom. I've thought deeply about this analogy, and now

I see it differently. Crabs in the bottom of a barrel aren't holding each other back out of spite—they're only hoping to get up and out. They're desperate and afraid. They want to get out of the barrel and get back to where they truly belong. They cling to the one who's closest to escaping, hoping for their own survival.

I view people latching onto me in the same way. They're not trying to hinder me or hold me back in some fashion; they're seeking a way out of their situation, or they need guidance and information they can't find in their current surroundings. Helping them brings me joy, because I believe the more we all live by Proverbs 27:17, the better the world becomes. This way we can latch together and stand stronger as one.

Two examples come to mind when I think of this verse. First, my hometown mentor, Mario "Jug" Mitchell—*rest in peace*. He gave me advice and let me "borrow some sense" by sharing lessons from his own past mistakes. He didn't spare me any stories or examples for his own benefit; he was simply always honest about his life. The lessons he taught me turned out to be some of the most vital lessons of my entire life. When I went to college, he stepped in financially a number of times when I needed help. Whether it was because I had too many parking tickets or if my car needed fixing. Once when the alternator on my old 1987 Chevy Caprice went out, he stepped in so he could save me and my mother from unnecessary stress. He not only showed me exactly what iron sharpening iron looks like—he exemplified it.

The second example is Bryan Cranston. While filming *Your Honor*, he asked me a couple simple questions, "What is your favorite genre? What kind of actor do you see yourself as?"

I said, "I prefer drama or suspense genres for both."

He challenged me to think differently saying, "I'm gonna ask you the same question tomorrow. Think about it tonight. I want you to give me a different answer when I ask you again."

I was baffled. I really didn't know how to answer the question. I thought maybe I had done something wrong.

The next day he asked me the same question, "So, what is your favorite genre and role to play?"

"I really don't have a different answer," I replied.

Then he explained to me something I will never forget. "I see something different in you. I've seen a glimpse of your work from another project. You are capable of doing a number of different types of characters. Never voluntarily put yourself into a box. This industry wants us in one, but it's definitely not necessary."

From that moment on I knew how to better vocalize the type of actor that I longed to be. That conversation confirmed my potential and taught me how to carry myself and embrace my journey as an actor. From his advice I learned how to present myself to the world and strive for greatness.

If Bryan were to ask me that question again today, I would answer, "I'm an actor with a unique instrument, and I possess the ability to perform whatever I so choose."

Proverbs 27:17 is more than a verse—it's a principle. When we help each other grow, hold each other accountable, and share knowledge, we all become stronger.

# PRINCIPLE #38

## Unlearn to Relearn

*"The definition of insanity is doing the same thing over and over and expecting different results."* —Albert Einstein

Unlearning to relearn is a foreign concept for many people. For those who are familiar with it, the process can still feel like an almost impossible task. Like Aristotle said, "We are what we repeatedly do. Excellence, then, is not an act, but a habit." Research says that if you do something only 20 to 30 times it's probably going to form a habit that will stick. That's exactly what happens in life—we spend years doing things we've been taught, and over time, they become second nature. Many times we don't ever question *why* we are doing what we're doing because it's just the way it's always been.

Most of us spend years, even decades, doing things we've been taught. Our behaviors may stem from what has been passed down for generations. Our culture and personal experience add to this, too. What happens when you reach a point in your life where you realize some of your habits or beliefs might no longer serve you? Maybe you're trying to accomplish something new, or you've come to understand that some part of your life needs to change. At that moment, you're faced with the challenge of breaking habits that have been deeply ingrained over time.

Actively breaking old patterns and beliefs is not easy for most people. As the old saying goes, "You can't teach an old dog new tricks."

Actually, you can teach an old dog new tricks, but it's just extremely hard. Research backs up this idea, it's called neuroplasticity. This is the brain's ability to reorganize itself and form new neural connections. John Hopkins University shows us that consistent practice and deliberate learning can help people of any age form new habits and perspectives.

I've had to unlearn and relearn many things throughout my life. One of the most challenging things for me was when I went to college and began taking communication classes. My professor told me, "If you're going into mass communications or broadcasting, you'll probably need a speech coach to help with your dialect and diction."

For an 18-year-old who has spoken the same way his entire life, it was difficult to hear. Actually, doing it was even harder. I started working with a coach who guided me through exercises to refine my speech. She wanted to help me grow—not destroy or bury who I was or how I spoke, but to add to my abilities. She helped me speak in different ways that would serve me in my future.

This unlearning and relearning now serve me on a daily basis. As an actor, those lessons were invaluable. I can now confidently speak in multiple dialects, expressing myself with clarity in each one. What once felt like a terrible and almost painful process turned out to be a blessing in disguise. It all came down to repetition and persistence. In his book *Atomic Habits*, James Clear explains, "You do not rise to the level of your goals; you fall to the level of your systems." Relearning is about rebuilding your systems.

Even as an adult, I've had to unlearn and relearn. Over the past few years, I've been confronting ideas and habits that no longer serve me. Because I've been through it before, I now see it as just a part of the growth process. When you challenge yourself to break old ideologies—whether about yourself, others, or the world—you open the door to continuous improvement.

The goal is always to grow, not just for yourself but for those around you. I challenge anyone who feels like they're hitting a brick wall or a dead end and you're at a place in your life where you want to pursue something new—a career, a journey, or a passion—to embrace the process of unlearning and relearning. Take the advice of Victor Frankl, "When we are no longer able to change a situation, we are challenged to change ourselves."

Whether it's knowledge about work, spirituality, politics, science, or anything else, if it's not serving you, let it go. Learn something that's a better fit for you, something that uplifts you and those around you. Growth is the reward, and it's always worth it.

# PRINCIPLE #39
## Spiritual Foundation

*"We can never obtain peace in the outer world
until we make peace with ourselves."*
—14th Dalai Lama, Tenzin Gyatso

I purposefully named this principle *Spiritual Foundation* because I don't want to give the impression that I favor one religion over another or believe there's a single "correct" religion. As an adult, I've embraced practices from various faiths, even incorporating some different elements that resonate with me into my daily life.

Growing up in Alabama, people might assume I'm Baptist, and while there are Baptist churches in my family history, I actually grew up attending a Methodist church. Christianity was all I knew until I went to college at the age of 18. There, I met people from other walks of life—those practicing Judaism, Buddhism, and many other faiths. I started opening myself to engaging in conversations with them. I asked them personal questions about their faith and their way of life. This opened my eyes to a common truth: at the very root of each religion lies love, sacrifice, structure, and faith.

It became clear to me that no matter what name is given to the Divine—God, Jehovah, Allah, YHWH, Buddha, Adonai, or the Messiah—the core principles are similar, no matter who you choose to worship. This realization has guided my spiritual journey and allowed me to explore different religious practices without losing my foundation.

Here's a simple, quick view of some similarities of the five major religions.

**Christianity:**
Emphasizes love, faith, compassion, and service. Promotes ethical living, moral standards, and connection to the Divine.
**Judaism:**
Focuses on covenant, justice, and community. Values love, ethical principles, moral standards, and connection to the Divine.
**Islam:**
Centers on submission to God, charity, and prayer. Highlights compassion, humility, and service to others.
**Hinduism:**
Advocates righteousness (dharma), mindfulness, and liberation. Encourages devotion to the Divine and respect for all life.
**Buddhism:**
Teaches mindfulness, compassion, and enlightenment. Promotes peace and alleviation of suffering.

As you can see at the very root of each religion there are basically the same principles. Across these religions, shared values such as compassion, love, ethical living, and devotion unite humanity. The Golden Rule, often phrased as "Treat others as you would like to be treated," is a universal concept found in all five religions. Mother Teresa said, *"The fruit of faith is love, and the fruit of love is service."* This interconnectedness between belief and action underscores how spirituality inspires us to lead lives filled with purpose, compassion, and contribution.

Just as all religions have similarities, there are some things in every religion that I agree with and some that I do not agree with. Through my spiritual journey, I've incorporated practices that might traditionally belong to other religions. For instance, yoga—often associated with Buddhism or Hinduism—has become an essential part of my life, even though some Christians view it skeptically. Likewise, praying at set times is usually associated with Muslims, but after studying the Bible closer for the last two years, and *unlearning and relearning*, I've read many passages about praying at set times during the day. Psalm 119:164, Acts 3:1, Exodus 29:39, and Luke 6:12 all speak of praying at designated times throughout the day.

Another pivotal moment in my spiritual journey was studying the Bible from a Hebrew perspective. This is extremely important because Jesus, originally known as Yeshua, was Hebrew. He had different customs and words than we use today. I even started learning some Hebrew words because of this. That way I could actually begin studying Hebrew texts. By doing this, I've found there are many more similarities within the Bible that relate to other religions. One that I had always questioned as a child was about the Sabbath being on the seventh day of the week. So why didn't we worship on Saturday, instead of Sunday? I realized that the Sabbath, as described in the Bible, aligns with Saturday—not Sunday. However, I also realized that whether I was observing it on Saturday or Sunday didn't matter because I wasn't doing it at the capacity that I should have been doing it. This conviction led me to begin honoring the Sabbath from sunset Friday to sunset Saturday, truly resting and dedicating that time to God.

This change wasn't easy. It required sacrifices, such as abstaining from work or even eating at restaurants, because I didn't want to support others working on the Sabbath. I basically use the time of the Sabbath as a true date for honoring God, resting, and rejuvenating my body, mind, and spirit. I've found so much peace by making this sacrifice and observing the Sabbath for a full 24 hours. It's one of the most rewarding commitments I've ever made in my life.

I don't judge anyone who observes differently than I do. They can observe the way that is best for them and brings them closer to God and their higher, spiritual self. That's the beauty of this world we live in. There are so many different walks of life, and so many different beliefs, practices, and religions—but the root of them is always the same. Regardless of one's faith, having a spiritual foundation provides stability when life's tough times arise. As Dr. Martin Luther King, Jr. once said, *"Faith is taking the first step even when you don't see the whole staircase."* Faith provides a sense of direction, guiding us through when we have no answers and are uncertain how to proceed.

Everyone needs a spiritual foundation to fall back on. Building a spiritual foundation is not about perfection but persistence. As Mahatma Gandhi observed, *"You may never know what results come of your actions, but if you do nothing, there will be no result."* Spiritual practices—whether through prayer, meditation, or service—are a step toward creating meaningful change within ourselves and in the world around us. If you don't take any other advice from this book, take the advice in this chapter and decide which faith or spiritual background you are being pulled toward. Delve into that one whole-heartedly and make it the backbone of your journey through life.

# PRINCIPLE #40
## Borrow Some Sense

---

*"Learn from the mistakes of others. You can't live long enough to make them all yourself."* —Eleanor Roosevelt

---

I can't help but laugh every time I think about my grandmother's words: *"Sometimes it's best to borrow some sense than to buy some."* She'd say this to me, my two cousins Cicely and Angel, and my brother Terrell when we were growing up. Anytime one of us messed up, especially by making a mistake, someone else already made or one we'd been warned about—if we turned around and made the same mistake—she'd hit us with that line.

For years, I had no idea what she was talking about. I didn't understand what she meant, *"borrow some sense"*? It wasn't until I was around 17 or 18 that it finally clicked. What she was saying was simple but profound: it's better to learn from other people's mistakes than to go through the pain of making those same mistakes yourself. Instead of ignoring the lessons life presents us, we should pay attention to those around us and avoid their pitfalls. Make certain that you are making your own choices and not just lollygagging behind someone else.

Retired major league baseball pitcher Vernon Law is remembered not only for his skill on the field but also for his strong work ethic and leadership. He won the Cy Young Award in 1960 and helped lead the Pittsburgh Pirates to victory over the Yankees in the World Series that year. Also known as "The Deacon" because of his strong faith, he tells us, "Experience is a hard teacher because she gives the test first, and the lesson afterward. Watching others take the test can often teach you the same lesson with less pain." His words reflect the wisdom my grandmother was trying to instill in us.

When you "buy some sense," it means you've paid the price for your lesson, whether through heartbreak, failure, or loss. That pain often stays with you, teaching you not to repeat the same mistake. There's value in that—it's deeply personal, and the memory of the experience can guide you in the future.

But did you know that borrowing sense has actually been shown to be the wiser path? Research by Ayelet Fishbach and Lauren Eskreis-Winkler found that people usually learn more effectively from observing others' failures than from their own. This difference is attributed to ego and self-esteem concerns, people tend to remember their own successes but forget their own mistakes.

Otto von Bismarck had some hard advice, saying "Only a fool learns from his own mistakes. The wise man learns from the mistakes of others." When you borrow sense, you observe and learn from others' failures without putting yourself through the trauma. It saves you time, heartache, and energy. Borrowing sense isn't always easy because it requires humility and awareness, but it's a shortcut to wisdom that can spare you a world of trouble.

That said, there are times when "buying sense" has its place. For example, when learning a new skill, you often have to experience it yourself for it to stick. If someone explains how to surf, you might grasp their instructions, but the moment you actually get on the board, fall off, and then stand up successfully, it becomes part of your muscle memory. That's the positive side of buying sense—the lesson is now ingrained in your memory.

When it comes to life's bigger, more important lessons my grandmother's words hold true. If you see someone fail in a way that you can avoid, why not take their experience as a guide? As Mary Dove Smith used to say, *"Sometimes it's best to borrow some sense rather than buy it."*

# PRINCIPLE #41
## Philanthropy

*"You have not lived today until you have done something for someone who can never repay you."* —John Bunyan

Philanthropy stands as a cornerstone of humanity, and the word itself holds power. Many people have heard it, but not everyone understands it. Some may have never encountered the term, yet its meaning is crucial for everyone to grasp and comprehend. I first learned about philanthropy during my first year in college. My mentor, Jeff Davis, a former Clemson football player—who went on to play for the Tampa Bay Buccaneers—introduced me to the concept. Jeff, also known as *'The Judge,'* was deeply involved in community work, including mentoring young boys through programs like *Big Brothers* and *Call Me MISTER®*. His efforts in the *Call Me MISTER®* program even caught the attention of Oprah Winfrey, who featured him on her show to highlight the impactful work he was doing in South Carolina.

Even though Jeff had great success as a professional athlete, he felt something was missing. Then he joined the *"Call Me MISTER®"* program. *Call Me MISTER®* stands for *Men Instructing Students Toward Effective Role Models.* It addresses the need for African-American male role models in elementary schools. Jeff was inspired when he learned that there were more young Black men in prison than in college. He then took it upon himself to do whatever he could to help the program's mission of recruiting, training, and placing 200 African-American males as elementary school teachers in South Carolina.

It became a collaborative effort involving Clemson University and three historically Black colleges. The program provides scholarships and mentorship, enabling many participants to be the first in their families to attend college. By pairing trainees with experienced mentors and placing them in classrooms early, the program helps children see Black men in a new light—not as athletes or stereotypes, but as educators. Mr. Davis really emphasized that teaching is a profession of dignity and honor, with the power to inspire and uplift communities. Following recognition on *The Oprah Winfrey Show*, the *Call Me MISTER®* program gained nationwide attention, using its $100,000 Use Your Life Award to fund scholarships and guide other schools in replicating its success.

One day I decided to ask *'The Judge'* if he could tell me more about his experiences of "giving back." That's when he used the term *philanthropy* and then he told me he was a *philanthropist*. I asked him if he could go into more details and wondered how I could become a philanthropist.

"A philanthropist is someone who wants to help promote the welfare of others," was his reply. "Most people do this by donating large sums of money, but there is another way of helping others that may even make more of an immediate difference."

Now I was intrigued because at the time, being a college student, I really didn't have the resources to donate large sums of money, but I really liked the idea of becoming a philanthropist—someone helping promote the welfare of others.

He continued, "Philanthropy isn't limited to financial contributions. You can also give your time. This can become very valuable to the person on the receiving end. When you give your time, it's a priceless gift—one that can leave a lasting impression long after monetary donations fade from memory. People may forget the $100 donation, but they won't forget the impactful moment that they had with you. Maybe you shared some words of wisdom or encouraged them, and that made all the difference in their world."

His wisdom resonated all the way down to the deepest part of my soul. I immediately knew that being a philanthropist was part of why I was here on this earth. I knew that number one was to worship and honor God and that number two was to honor Him through our actions of how we treat one another.

Eagerly I asked, "What are some ways that I can become a philanthropist now, in my first year of college, even though I don't have any money?"

"You can start by using your platform. Share your unique experiences. Share the knowledge that you have that others may lack. Many times, younger people just need leadership and guidance. Spending time with them and motivating them to do the right thing can change every aspect of their lives. Then when you get to a place where you can do things financially, you just add that to the equation."

I was encouraged by his words and immediately started seeking out ways to help at a high level. Following his guidance, I sought out Kathy Cauthen, a campus leader at Clemson University who was deeply involved in community service. Kathy connected me with local initiatives where I began mentoring children who needed positive influences in their lives. This became the foundation of my journey into philanthropy.

Over time, I expanded my efforts. Today, I give back in many ways: donating clothes and money to group homes and homeless shelters, feeding the homeless, and mentoring in youth centers, high schools, detention centers, and even prisons. I also contribute my time, voice, and financial resources to churches. I'm always open to suggestions when it comes to different ways to pour my resources into people. These acts may vary in scale, but they share one common goal—making a difference in someone's life.

I'm not big on broadcasting that I help people in their time of need, so the majority of the deeds I do for individuals, I do in private. I embrace Matthew 6: 1-4, which reads, "But when you give to the needy, do not let your left hand know what your right hand is doing, so that your giving may be in secret. Then your Father, who sees what is done in secret, will reward you." I truly believe when things are done privately, they remain pure and authentic. Of course, there are efforts we publicize for the betterment of a program, a Non-profit, etc. But when possible, remember this passage.

I believe that if you change just one life, you change the world. You don't have to change millions of lives to make a difference. Changing millions is something I strive to do because it's far more impactful, but the moment you change one life, you never know how that person will end up helping others, or even you. Those ripples will extend far beyond the two of you.

I often wear a gold chain that was gifted to me. On the chain is a domino charm. Oftentimes people will notice it and ask something along the lines, "Are you a big fan of the game Dominoes?" My answer is always, "Yes, I am, but that's not the message behind this particular charm. The designer created it as a reminder that every great deed done leads to a domino effect of the same." The necklace serves as a reminder for me.

I encourage everyone, no matter your financial status or geographic location, to find ways to give back. Whether through time, knowledge, or resources, becoming a philanthropist is within reach for us all. As Winston Churchill famously said, *"We make a living by what we get, but we make a life by what we give."* I hope I've inspired you to give generously and purposefully. And then you, like me, will become a philanthropist.

# PRINCIPLE #42

## Patience Before Progress

*"Patience and perseverance have a magical effect before which difficulties disappear and obstacles vanish."* —John Quincy Adams

Patience is a virtue often overlooked in today's fast-paced "microwave society," where instant gratification has become the norm. Answers to your wildest questions can be answered in seconds—a mere click away. Packages from Amazon arrive within just one or two days after placing an order. This is much different than when I was a child; I used to order my shoes from a magazine called *Eastbay*. It would take 10 days for my order to come through.

The convenience we enjoy today has inadvertently fostered impatience, particularly in younger generations who are now accustomed to immediate results when it comes to creating, achieving, or finishing something. For most, the longest thing that they've had to do or endure is literally going through 12 to 13 years of schooling to make it to their graduation ceremony. Most other things in their lives are "microwaved" with quick solutions and instant gratification becoming all they know, leaving little room for the patience and persistence required to achieve long-term goals.

Many things have changed in the last century or two. The evolution of how we access information and receive packages has both benefits and drawbacks. The internet offers instant information, but often at the cost of depth, reliability, and critical thinking. In September of 2023, the OxJournal.org stated that the rise of digital technology, especially the internet, has significantly impacted attention spans, particularly among younger generations. The constant stream of information and digital multitasking involved in internet use can hinder the brain's ability to maintain sustained focus. Studies suggest that online activities, from social media use to browsing content, encourage rapid shifts in attention, which reduces a person's capacity to concentrate for long periods of time. This phenomenon has been linked to a decreased patience when it comes to the ability of focusing on tasks that require sustained mental effort.

However, as I've learned throughout my life, the importance of patience remains undeniable. Today I truly appreciate how my guardians and mentors were so patient with me while I was learning and growing. In high school, my struggle with patience became evident when I found myself retaking some classes during my senior year to boost my GPA for college eligibility.

One of those classes was 9th-grade English. This happened because I had become too comfortable with doing just enough to get by—it came back to bite me. As a high-profile football player, the experience was humbling, especially when you're surrounded by a classroom full of freshmen. Miss Talaya Williams, my English teacher, was informed about my situation. She knew that I needed to make an A in her class to get my GPA where it needed to be. I was pretty quiet in her class at first. I was a little embarrassed because of me being a high school football star—everyone knew my name and probably guessed the reason I was in that class.

A few days later, that shyness started wearing off, and it wasn't long before I regained my natural personality of confidence and humor, which naturally drew attention from my classmates. A lot of them were asking me questions and basically following in my footsteps. Everything I would do they would do.

Miss Williams recognized my situation and asked me to stay after class one day. She gave me an extended talk and took the time to help me realize the significance of leadership and how important it was for me to set a good example for others to follow. One of the things she said to me, I'll never forget, "Be the version of yourself now, that the 21-year-old you can appreciate later."

She taught me about staying focused to make sure I achieved—and most importantly *earned*—the A that I needed in her class. She said to me, "When you finish this class, I will either be your worst enemy in the world, or your favorite person. One way or another I will see to it that you earn your A."

At that moment I knew she would probably be my favorite person, because I was all about respect. I was about putting skin in the game. I was about genuine love. Her taking the time to have that conversation with me and showing me her unwavering support, patience, and interest in my future motivated me to rise to the occasion. I immediately respected her at a level that no other teacher had earned from me in the past.

By the end of the semester, I not only earned an A but gained a true and profound respect for her dedication. Miss Williams cried the day grades came out. She looked at me and said, "You earned this," with pride beaming from her face. Her patience taught me that growth requires time, effort, and selflessness. She taught me by example that by sticking to a plan, being who I truly am, homing in and staying focused I can achieve anything. She also taught me that a true leader leads by example and not just words.

The amount of patience Miss Talaya Williams had for me during that class was exactly what I needed at that moment. She really didn't have to have that sort of patience with me. Many times, when we are dealing with things that aren't directly affecting us, we are completely impatient. We want the people we are teaching to just get it already. We want them to hurry up and understand or figure it out. When we do this, we may inadvertently discourage the very people we are trying to help. Whether it's our peers, friends, students, children, or mentees who give a helping hand, love and patience will immediately make it easier for that person to do whatever it is they're intending to do.

I've witnessed people practicing patience through farmers, coaches, doctors, chiropractors, therapists, girlfriends, my guardians, my mentors and of course, my mother. All of these people have had amplified patience with me so that I would progress. This is a form of being selfless. We have to apply this quality to our own personal lives.

Most importantly, we have to allow ourselves the time to mature and grow. Progress will come if we take the time to grab ideas, to develop skills, and to learn what is needed. "If one advances confidently in the direction of his dreams, and endeavors to live the life which he has imagined, he will meet with a success unexpected in common hours," that's what the legendary Henry David Thoreau tells us. In time things will unfold naturally, and we will see that the success we were trying to achieve has come. All because patience comes before progress.

# PRINCIPLE #43

## Belief and Faith; a Beautiful Duo

---

*"Whether you think you can, or you think you can't, you're right."* —Henry Ford

---

If you believe you can accomplish something, you're more likely to take the steps necessary to succeed. If you don't believe you can accomplish something, you've probably already failed before you've started. As our opening quote states, in both cases you are right. Almost everything in life begins with belief. Whether consciously or not, belief and faith are at the core of our actions. Consider the simple act of getting out of bed. Each morning, we place our feet on the ground with the faith that our legs will support us and carry us forward. There's no disbelief, it's not a thought we dwell on because we've done it countless times before. This quiet confidence—born of repeated experiences—symbolizes the foundation of faith we need in all aspects of life.

We're all works in progress. I am no different than you, I have to remind myself constantly to believe. Whenever my faith tends to waiver, I try remembering something from my past that God has given me the strength to do or overcome. I tell myself; *He's done it before—He'll do it again.* When it comes to bigger goals and challenges, belief must work hand in hand with faith. It's natural to face doubts, but reminding ourselves of past successes can anchor our trust in what's possible.

## BELIEF AND FAITH; A BEAUTIFUL DUO

I remember the first time I went surfing in Los Angeles. At a height of six foot, seven inches and weighing 305 pounds, with knees that have been put to the test during my football career, I doubted my ability before I even set foot on the board.

My friend, Giovanni, was my instructor. He looked at me before we started and said, "You know, once you get this, you're probably going to be the biggest surfer in the world."

We laughed and I replied, "You, know—it's probably going to be pretty difficult. I'm a big guy, and my knees aren't so good."

"You'll figure it out," he replied.

He took me out into the ocean and taught me one of the first steps of surfing. Then a second step, and a third. I failed time and time again, never really getting off my stomach without falling in the water.

I went home later that day and replayed everything over in my mind. I remembered saying, "It's gonna be difficult for me," before I even attempted to surf. All of a sudden a wave of truth came crashing down upon me: *Whether you think you can or you think you can't—you are right.* I felt things begin to shift.

The following week Giovanni said, "You've got one day under your belt. You'll be a better surfer today."

This time I said something a lot different than the last time, "Yeah! Man, I'm gonna get it today. I've got faith. I believe it."

That day I stood up on the board on my second attempt. Even though I only stood for about two seconds riding the wave—I immediately felt one with the earth. It was one of the most exhilarating feelings I'd ever experienced as an adult. Something shifted when I decided to change my mindset. That small victory began with the simple decision to believe.

This was just something simple like a hobby, but when you take that mindset and you implement the idea of believing that you can do something, then have faith that God is going to help you achieve it, there's no telling what you can accomplish. Unfortunately, humans are wired to prioritize negative outcomes because our ancestors needed to focus on threats to survive. It was important for them to be attuned to danger and potential failure to avoid risks that could have been life-threatening. Studies show people fear losses more than they value gains. This fear can lead to putting more focus on what might go wrong rather than what could go right.

You may have been conditioned from a very young age to focus on avoiding making mistakes, rather than embracing opportunities. Traditional education often puts more emphasis on the errors you make rather than encouraging a child's creativity or risk-taking. In the Gospel of Matthew, even Christ's very own disciples did not believe in themselves. In Matthew 17:20 the Messiah says, "Because of your lack of faith, I tell you this: if you have faith as small as a mustard seed, you could tell a mountain to move from here to there, and it would move. Nothing would be impossible for you."

If you're not sure how big a mustard seed is, it's about the same size as a poppy seed you might find on a hamburger bun. The tiny mustard seed grows quickly into a shrub that can reach 6-10 feet in height in one season. Your faith, which may seem insignificant to you, is anything but. When it is nurtured, the results can be incredible. You only need a tiny amount of faith for God to help you accomplish something great.

Fear is often the greatest obstacle. Throughout our lives, fear is instilled in us by experiences, conversations, and others' doubts. It is easy to begin adopting the belief that certain things are impossible because we or others before us have failed. We must reject these imposed fears and eliminate those thoughts. Limitations do not define our potential.

Remember this: every failure is simply a lesson. Each mistake provides valuable knowledge about what works and what doesn't. These lessons aren't roadblocks; they're steppingstones to your next victory. With belief, faith, and the courage to persevere, anything is possible. So believe…

# PRINCIPLE #44
## It's a Marathon, Not a Sprint

> *"The marathon continues, we're just getting started. The marathon is about keeping going, staying on the path no matter how hard it gets."* —Nipsey Hussle

According to legend, Pheidippides was a herald sent from the battlefield near the town of Marathon to Athens to deliver the news of a Greek victory over the invading Persian army. This was a pivotal conflict in which the Greeks were totally outnumbered by their adversary. It is said that Pheidippides ran approximately 25 miles from Marathon to Athens without stopping. Upon arriving, he burst into the Athenian assembly saying, "Νενικήκαμεν!" (meaning—We have won!), and then he collapsed and died from exhaustion. Pheidippides' run symbolized the Greeks' determination and unity of their country over any external threats.

Inspired by the ancient legend, the modern marathon race was introduced in 1896 as an event in the first contemporary Olympic Games held in Athens, Greece. It was later standardized to a longer distance of 26.2 miles (42.195 kilometers) in the 1908 London Olympics to accommodate the British royal family's request to have the race start at Windsor Castle and finish in front of the royal box at the Olympic stadium.

Since then, the marathon has become a global symbol of endurance, perseverance, and the human spirit's ability to overcome challenges. It's a grueling commitment to run 26.2 miles and experienced runners will tell you that many times while running the mind and body often play tricks on you. This happened to producer Will Packer during a recent marathon in D.C. Even though he faced significant hurdles—like getting sick before the race, needing an IV just to start, cramping up, and even stopping to lay down at times—he pushed through.

He described the mental battles he faced when he wanted to give up as his mind tried coping with his body's exhaustion and the constant interplay between physical and mental endurance. His race is a reflection of life itself: along the path to achieving any significant goal, we encounter emotional, mental, and physical obstacles. It's vital to resist the urge to view ourselves as victims, and just quit. Understand instead that these challenges are part of the journey.

Airmiess Joseph Asghedom was born on August 15, 1985. He is known professionally as Nipsey Hussle—an American rapper, entrepreneur, and activist. He grew up in South Central Los Angeles not too far from the famous cross section of Slauson and Crenshaw, one of the most dangerous areas in L.A. At the tender age of 14, Airmiess left home and joined the local Rollin' 60s Neighborhood Crips, a subgroup of the larger Crips gang based in his home neighborhood of Crenshaw.

Only three short years after leaving home, Airmiess joined Buttervision, a creative multimedia movement led by Dexter Browne. During this time, an acquaintance gave him the name Nipsey Hussle (after the famous comedian, Nipsey Russell) because of his work ethic. It didn't take long and Nipsey was contributing to projects such as the *BV Boys Sampler*, *Beats & Babes*, and *Shades of Butter*.

Nipsey became known in his hometown as the cornerstone or the backbone of the Slauson/Crenshaw intersection, where he opened his clothing store *Marathon* giving back to the community from where he came. The store became a hub for promoting community empowerment and innovation, blending fashion with technology. Nipsey used it as an example of how to integrate purpose into business endeavors, inspiring others to keep pushing forward, no matter the circumstances

He named his brand *Marathon* because of his unique way of viewing life. It represented the long and deliberate process of changing his own life. He knew that changing his habits, circumstances, and image would take time, discipline, and resilience. He once remarked in an interview that his success wasn't due to being better than anyone else but rather because he refused to give up. Also saying, "That's why the *Marathon* brand means so much to me, because I knew it wasn't going to be a sprint; it's a continued marathon." This mindset and message resonated deeply with many people all over the world. Highlighting the importance of embracing life's journey, learning from hardships, and staying committed to long-term aspirations which are at the core of every human spirit.

Unfortunately, on March 31, 2019, the world lost Nipsey Hussle. He was gunned down and murdered right in front of his *Marathon* clothing store. Nipsey's passing was a devastating blow to the world, but especially to the community he worked tirelessly to uplift. He was a beacon of hope for many people living in that area, inspiring countless young people of color to believe in themselves, pursue their dreams, and never give up.

Thousands filled the streets, including myself, to honor his legacy, our grief shining as a testament to his profound influence on the community he loved and empowered. This outpouring of honor and affection concluded with a memorial service at the 20,000-seat Staples Center, where fans, friends, and family gathered to celebrate a life dedicated to inspiring change and fostering hope. His final ride in the hearse was 26 miles around Los Angeles. I stood by around mile seven to pay my respects. Though his life was cut short, his legacy continues to shine for us all.

Like many of you, I can personally relate to Nipsey and his concepts. Even though my background wasn't nearly as harsh, dangerous, and severe as his—we both have one thing in common—starting from ground zero. Figuring out my purpose on this earth and how to achieve it has been a marathon in itself. It's taken years to get where I am, and I know I have years ahead to reach where I want to be.

I knew that by adopting the Gen Z "microwave mentality" and expecting instantaneous results, like the famous slogan from *J. G. Wentworth*, "It's my money, and I want it now," would not take me where I wanted to go. Instead, I embraced the trials and tribulations, taking each step deliberately and allowing the journey to shape me. Rather than viewing my challenges as hindrances or thinking that things aren't unfolding fast enough, I see the process as essential for growth.

This mindset applies to anyone with big aspirations. Luke 12:48 tells us: Everyone who has been given much, much will be demanded; and from the one who has been entrusted with much, much more will be asked. Reaching great heights, like Nipsey's clothing and record brand, demands endurance, lessons, and appreciation for the journey. There are things you have to go through in order to be ready once you reach your goal. Understand that each step shapes us into who we need to be to sustain and appreciate our accomplishments. It's a universal message for anyone pursuing big dreams.

Throughout history, people of all races and walks of life have had to endure oppressive situations and tough realities. Because I'm from the African American community, I'm attuned to the deep and penetrating struggle of my people and what they have faced in the last 400 plus years, but every now and then someone emerges and rises above the struggle. A spirit is sent to us by God, teaching valuable lessons through their life on Earth. Communicating not just by their words but through their actions as well. Many of them have had untimely deaths like Nipsey Hussle—such as Dr. Martin Luther King, Jr., Malcolm X,

Fred Hampton, Tupac, and Bob Marley, but their legacies endure. Even Nelson Mandela, although he lived to be 95 and was from South Africa, taught us many valuable lessons we can apply to our lives.

If I were to sum up the lives and contributions from these men it would be a reminder that no matter where we start or what obstacles we face, we can rise to great heights. Their lives show that through diligence, focus, and perseverance, we can achieve far more than statistics or others may tell us. Their stories are all marathons of life.

This philosophy aligns with the challenges faced in a literal marathon, where each mile tests the body and mind differently. Life's trials and difficulties aren't roadblocks—they're opportunities to grow and prepare for greater achievements. You must have a "never give up" attitude combined with patience, faith, and dedication.

While the historical accuracy of Pheidippides' run is debated, the myth remains an inspiring legacy that binds the ancient and modern worlds across time and generations. Along life's journey, obstacles will come, but it's essential to remember that it's not us against the world. Instead, every challenge we face is shaping us and preparing us for the destination we've set out to reach. When we emerge from the trials, we'll have more gratitude for the journey, a deeper sense of accomplishment, and a wealth of experiences to share.

Tough times are inevitable, but you must remember that the greatest untapped potential often lies in the graveyard—where people gave up before realizing their full potential. As long as you have breath in your lungs and blood pumping through your veins, your marathon continues. By having faith, patience, and perseverance, you can achieve anything.

# PRINCIPLE #45
## Celebrate Every Victory

*"Success is the sum of small efforts, repeated day in and day out."* —Robert Collier

There is great importance in celebrating victories—every single one of them. All too often, we focus only on chasing our ultimate goals and overlook the small wins along the way. In reality, what may seem small compared to the end goal is massive when measured against where we began. This comparison can be related to *The Law of Relativity*. Whether we're speaking in physics or life philosophy, *The Law of Relativity* essentially means that everything we experience is relative to our perspective, comparison, or frame of reference.

In life philosophy, *The Law of Relativity* is often interpreted as a principle that teaches us to see all circumstances in context. Our perception of a situation's difficulty or significance is relative to the comparisons we make—such as to past experiences, others' lives, or imagined ideals. By shifting perspectives, we can find gratitude and growth in seemingly small victories. Whether it's mastering a new skill, reaching a new level, or simply moving one step closer to our goal, every accomplishment deserves gratitude and acknowledgment.

Learning to embrace your victories and be grateful for them—big or small—is truly important. It's something I personally have struggled with and have reminded myself to do. Thankfully, I've gotten better over the last couple of years, because what usually happens when we accomplish something is we forget about it. It's over and done with, and we automatically start looking on to what we have to do next. We immediately start asking subconscious questions like: How can I get even better? What do I need to do next? How can I get closer to my ultimate goal? These are all good questions to help us get to the next level but take time to congratulate yourself and send up some gratitude for what you've accomplished.

Gratitude plays a necessary role in how high you climb the ladder of life. As the saying goes, "Gratitude affects your altitude." The more you express appreciation for what you've achieved, the more the universe aligns to bring you more of what you value—and the higher you'll go. Celebrating your victories doesn't mean extravagant displays of champagne showers or luxury vacations—it can be as simple as taking a moment to reflect, thank God, the universe, and those who helped you: a coach, teacher, friend, or mentor.

Never downplay or minimize your accomplishments. Think about the Great Pyramids. They are by all standards simply magnificently designed and are true world wonders. They are so impressive that it is hard for most people to grasp the vastness of their architecture and the precision of their alignment. To this day they continue to mystify modern-day observers.

However, if you were to look at one stone alone, it may seem insignificant, but when you look at all the stones together, they form a masterpiece. The Great Wall of China is another great example. One stone from the Great Wall may not look like much, but when they are all put together you can see the Great Wall from space, under the right conditions.

It took stone after stone after stone to make those mammoth monuments. Each and every stone was needed for stability. Taking just one for granted could cause the whole thing to crumble. Each step in life works the same way. Skipping even one phase of progress can lead to instability later. Some people achieve success quickly and seem to skip all the steps, going from ground zero to 100, but without the foundational tools learned along the way through experience, they often break down from stress or fail to sustain their success.

A good example of this is from *USA Today*, July 20, 2023. The piece states that "nearly one-third of lottery winners eventually go bankrupt within three to five years. Which means they are more likely than the average American to file bankruptcy…" Why? Financial mismanagement, extravagant spending, poor investments, and pressure from friends and family often contribute to this rapid depletion of wealth, because the winners have not had life lessons on how to govern that much money.

Sometimes you may look at certain people and think, *how did they do that?* It seems as though they got there by doing nothing. But you really have no idea what they have done behind the scenes. You may not have a clue of how hard they worked, or what they sacrificed to get to that point.

Dabo Swinney, my old college coach, used to say, "There's no elevator to success. You always have to take the stairs." That lesson stuck with me. Anytime I feel tempted to take a shortcut, I remind myself that those skipped steps often hold the keys to sustaining and building success. So, I stretch my hamstrings, tighten my shoelaces, and take the first step.

Cherish each and every victory. Each step along the way is important to the climb itself. Celebrate each step, reflect on how far you've come, and keep moving forward with gratitude as your guide.

# PRINCIPLE #46
## The Power of Words and Energy

---

*"Words are free. It's how you use them that may cost you."* —KushandWizdom

---

Most of us take for granted how powerful our words really are. Many whose faith follows the Bible are familiar with Proverbs 18:21, even if they may not recognize it as a reminder of the power source we have over our lives: "The tongue has the power of life and death, and those who love it will eat its fruit." This verse highlights the profound impact that words can have, either bringing life through encouragement and kindness, or causing harm through negativity and destructive speech.

The verse is often interpreted as a reminder of the responsibility we have with our words, encouraging people to speak thoughtfully and use their speech to uplift others. It emphasizes the idea that the consequences of our words extend beyond the moment they are spoken, affecting not only ourselves but also those around us.

Proverbs 16:24 also reminds us, "Gracious words are a honeycomb, sweet to the soul and healing to the bones." Our words can either heal or curse others and ourselves. From the moment we open our eyes, we must be conscious of our thoughts and, more importantly, what comes from our lips. Even small things, like saying "I'm coming down with a cold" or "I feel myself getting sick" can affect our health. Just because our immune system is a little off doesn't mean we need to claim that sickness; we have time to correct it before we speak negativity over it. We could say instead, "I'm starting to feel better today." The moment we say something negative or positive, we're setting that course in motion.

This principle applies not only to health but to all areas of our lives. Phrases like "When it rains, it pours," or "If it ain't one thing, it's another," are often said out of habit, but they only attract more of the same negative energy. These are things we've been programmed to say, and they can perpetuate the negative situations we experience.

We find references throughout the entire Bible (*Basic Instructions Before Leaving Earth*) warning us and reminding us that our words hold great and wondrous power. In the book of James we are given the metaphor about the rudder of a ship and your tongue highlighting the influence our words can have. James 3:4-5 says, "Look also at ships: although they are so large and are driven by fierce winds, they are turned by a very small rudder wherever the pilot desires. Even so the tongue is a little member and boasts great things. Consider how an entire forest can be set on fire by a tiny flame!" In Colossians 3:17 we are told, "And whatever you do, whether in word or deed, do it all in the name of Christ…"

When we live among others, the energy we bring into those spaces is just as important as our words. If you carry ill intentions or negative thoughts, that energy will affect those around you. Similarly, if you're surrounded by people with low energy, they can drain you if you're not careful. That's why it's important to stay mindful of the energy we carry and protect ourselves from negative influences.

Affirming ourselves with positive words is a wonderful practice to implement into your daily life. You've probably heard of affirmations—repeating positive statements about yourself like "I am strong," "I am healthy," "I am wealthy," "I am a leader, "Everything I touch turns to gold." These statements are not just about convincing ourselves but also about putting those intentions into the universe. As we speak these things, we invite them into our lives. By focusing on positive affirmations, we can help counterbalance any negativity we might express unintentionally.

Think of how wonderful it would be if all of us could get our negative thoughts and words down to zero, but we are human and imperfect so sometimes we slip up and say things we don't necessarily mean or want. We must be constantly vigilant and continuously practicing positive affirmations, words, and thoughts over ourselves and those around us.

It's also essential to hold others accountable for their words. In Proverbs 27:17, it says, "As iron sharpens iron, so one person sharpens another." If someone speaks negatively about us, we need to challenge those words. I don't like it when people say to me, "I saw that little clip you did" or "How about that little accomplishment you had?" I often will say in return, "Hey, please don't refer to (whatever accomplishment) as being little. It's a big thing, something that's going to create many more opportunities for me. Please don't speak that over me." Another thing I will not allow is negative teasing or joking. I'll say something like, "Don't speak that over me, because even if you're joking the universe doesn't know how to take a joke, and it's already working to send that back to me."

When we are parents, watching our words and energy is even more important because our children are soaking up everything we say and do as fast as a dry sponge in a bowl full of water. Again, we can refer back to the Bible, Deuteronomy 6:7 is referring to God's commandments: "Impress them on your children. Talk about them when you sit at home and when you walk along the road, when you lie down and when you get up." This reflects the principle of speaking and doing good things at all times.

When you start saying more positive things and bringing more positive energy to your family and friends, they begin following your lead, because they notice how your life seems to be a little better or even a lot better than their own. I remember when I was 14, I told my family

I wasn't going to say "bye" anymore because I didn't like how I felt when I said it. It gave me the feeling of being too final. It seemed like I was saying, "Okay, farewell—nice knowing you." I took the word "bye" out of my vocabulary and instead, I started saying, "See you later" or "Talk to you soon" or "I love you" because I didn't want to imply that our connections were over and final. Little changes like this can have a big impact on how we feel and how we communicate with others.

Over the years, I've taken several words out of my speech. You have to listen to your heart and decide what feels good for you to say or not to say. You are protecting yourself and others by being conscious of where exactly your tongue is leading you.

Indeed, our words hold great power, but there are other ways of bringing good energy into your life. Keep in mind, however, that even though the Bible acknowledges the beauty and significance of creation, it warns us against idolizing physical objects. Nonetheless, there are many ways to use the beautiful creations of God to uplift us and create a harmonious environment around us.

Many things on this earth—like plants, herbs, and stones—can positively influence our energy. We have the right to decide what we allow in our space to support our well-being. Whether it's a plant in the room or a specific practice, choosing what adds life to our environment and helps to elevate us is key.

Compare for a moment how you feel when walking down a city street with tall, ugly, unkempt buildings and dirty streets in contrast to walking down a street that is clean and tidy with beautiful, architecturally pleasing buildings and massive, old trees lining the streets. I can't think of one person on earth that would choose ugliness over beauty. Truly the energy in your environment cannot be denied. Our external surroundings profoundly shape our internal states, emphasizing the importance of designing spaces that add positivity to our daily experiences.

Old churches and buildings were purposefully designed with sacred geometry, gemstones, and intricate architecture to evoke feelings of upliftment and spiritual connection. They incorporated sacred geometry, beauty, and harmony into every design. Sacred geometry combines mathematical ratios and patterns, such as the golden ratio and Fibonacci sequence, which are often seen in nature.

These designs are thought to resonate with our subconscious understanding of universal order, creating a sense of peace and harmony. Many sacred structures, from Gothic cathedrals to Islamic mosques, use these principles to evoke awe and contemplation. Gemstones used in religious and sacred spaces are believed to enhance energy and connection to the divine. Materials like marble, quartz, and other precious stones reflect light beautifully, creating an ethereal atmosphere. Symbolically, they can represent purity, eternity, and spiritual enlightenment.

We are deeply influenced by the elements we surround ourselves with—whether it's words, plants, herbs, stones, or other natural elements. Each of these has unique properties that can harmonize energy and protect us against negativity. Research shows that specific plants purify the air and uplift our mood, certain herbs have calming or invigorating effects, and stones like quartz or amethyst are believed to emit energy that fosters clarity, balance, or protection. By selecting your words and the elements around you with intention, you create an environment that nurtures not just your physical space but also your emotional and spiritual well-being.

# PRINCIPLE #47
## Toe the Line with Delusion

*"Therefore I tell you, whatever you ask in prayer, believe that you have received it, and it will be yours."* —Mark 11:24

This principle may be unexpected or even unfamiliar to many, but it's an essential skill we must refine if we want to manifest our dreams. The concept of manifestation, popularized by books like *The Secret*, taught me the importance of combining faith with a healthy amount of delusion.

Healthy delusion is the ability to believe so deeply in a vision that it feels real before it materializes. It's the ability to imagine, see, smell, and touch your goals as if they already exist. You close your eyes, meditate on them, and they feel tangible. It's about using your imagination. However, sharing this vision with the wrong person might give them cause to call you "delusional." That's why you have to "toe the line," having a delicate balance of faith and illusion and know just how far you can go.

Because I've played sports for a good portion of my life, I like the metaphor of "toeing the line." In football "toe the line" typically refers to a player positioning themselves precisely on or near a specific line on the field, such as the line of scrimmage or sideline, in accordance with the rules of the game to get as far as they possibly can. In life, "toe the line" means going as far as you can go and still adhering to rules, expectations, or standards set by society, authority figures, or oneself.

This can mean maintaining discipline, staying within boundaries, and meeting the demands or constraints of a given situation without crossing limits.

Faith + Illusion = Manifestation. You have to toe the line between these three. It's a delicate balance of belief, discernment and action. Faith is entrusting a higher power, the universe, or God to guide your steps, while manifestation requires aligning your mindset and actions toward your goals. These two must work in harmony, creating a "marriage" between belief and effort.

Unhealthy delusion, however, happens when someone dreams of greatness but refuses to act. They stay in the same job, live the same routine, and yet say things like, "When I get rich," without taking any steps to make it happen. Many times when people lose faith or hope in the things they want to manifest it's simply because their actions are not aligned with their intentions.

In contrast, when you have a healthy amount of faith in your delusions and goals it propels you to act as if your dreams are on their way. You already know something greater is on its way before having tangible proof. Faith that is rooted in trusting God, provides you with hope and perseverance. It offers peace, a steady mindset, and a state of being that is aligned with your actions and beliefs—that's when true manifestation occurs.

The passage of Philippians 4:6-7 commands us to "... not be anxious about anything, but in every situation, by prayer and petition, with thanksgiving, present your requests to God. And the peace of God, which transcends all understanding, will guard your hearts and your minds in Christ Jesus," highlighting the fact that peace comes from trusting in God's plan and feeling that peace, even as you make your requests known to Him.

Another key to successful manifestation is discretion. Not every dream needs to be shared with the world. As Robert Greene advises in *The 48 Laws of Power*, "Conceal your intentions." When you reveal your plans to the wrong people, they may project negativity, calling you delusional or dismissing your vision as being sheer fantasy. Some may even purposefully or inadvertently try hindering your plans. Remember, not everyone will support your path. For one reason or another they may not want you to succeed. Unnecessary external input can create barriers where none existed before. The energy and words of unsupportive people have the power to derail your focus and dilute your manifestation if you're not diligent.

There are enough trials, tribulations, and barriers before getting what you desire without adding outside sources that will hinder you more. Instead, keep your dreams close to home—between yourself, your vision board, your journal, God, and your meditations. You don't have to remain quiet. You can speak your vision aloud directly to yourself—believing it, and feeling it. This allows your desires to remain pure and at the forefront of your mind. Neville Goddard tells us to, "Assume the feeling of the wish fulfilled and observe the route that your attention follows." This concept is in line with his central message: you must fully embody the feeling of your desired outcome as if it has already come to pass. This is part of the process of aligning your consciousness with your goals and desires. This is also called, "Feeling it forward."

Manifestation requires faith, belief, action, and discipline to keep your dreams protected. By embracing a healthy amount of delusion and keeping your intentions focused, you can create the life you envision. Neville Goddard also stated, "To make your dreams come true, you must first live in the end of them. Feel the joy, the peace, the satisfaction, and let it radiate." And that, my friends, is how you "toe the line with delusion."

# PRINCIPLE #48

## Leave the Gavel to the Judge

*"Be curious, not judgmental."* —Walt Whitman

When it comes to the principle of withholding judgment, my grandmother got it right when she said, "Leave the gavel to the judge." I've excelled in this area for most of my life. I've rarely been one to judge people quickly. In fact, I've always felt I had a "superpower" when it comes to the ability of viewing situations from someone else's perspective. I believe that people who rush to judgment lack this superpower, which can be labeled as empathy. Empathy is the ability to understand and share the feelings of another person. It involves recognizing emotions in others and being able to imagine what they might be experiencing or feeling, then responding with care and compassion.

Whenever you encounter someone whose behavior seems weird, unorthodox, or even offensive, instead of asking yourself, *"What's wrong with them?"* try asking, *"What happened to them?"* There are so many things that go into the presentation of every human you meet on a daily basis. People's actions often stem from past experiences—trauma, mental health challenges, or other unseen struggles. There's a complex story behind every person you meet and remembering that can help sustain the superpower of empathy when someone in your presence needs it.

Asking the question, "What is wrong?" comes from a judgmental place. Asking, "What happened to them?" comes from a place of caring and compassion. I've always admired how, in the Bible, when someone approached the Messiah, He would inquire rather than judge. He asked questions like "Why?" or "What happened?" before addressing their faith or the lack thereof. His approach showed a deep understanding and compassion for human struggles. He viewed everyone by looking at them through their spirit and not their external behaviors. He wanted to understand the deeper reasons behind their actions.

One of the most powerful illustrations of empathy and understanding is found in John 8:1-11 when He encounters a woman caught in adultery. Christ looks beyond societal judgment and focuses on restoration and compassion. The story goes like this:

A woman accused of adultery (a crime punishable by stoning according to the law of Moses) is brought before Yeshua (*Jesus*) by religious leaders. The leaders ask him whether she should be condemned, attempting to trap Him into either contradicting the law or appearing merciless.

Instead of immediately answering, Yeshua writes in the sand, as if He doesn't hear them. They continue to ask him. So, he stands and says, "Let any one of you who is without sin be the first to cast a stone at her." Then he bends down and continues writing in the sand, inviting the accusers to reflect upon their own conscience. This response shifts the focus from the woman's guilt to the accusers' self-examination, highlighting a universal need for grace.

Once they begin thinking about their own sins, one by one the accusers leave. He then stands back up and faces the woman with understanding and compassion. He does not condone her actions but neither does He condemn her. Instead, He says to her, "Woman, where are thine accusers? Hath no man condemned thee?"

"No one, my Lord," replies the woman.

The Messiah says, "Go now and sin no more."

His approach restores her dignity while encouraging her to change.

In my own journey to grow and become a better man than I was yesterday, I strive to keep this principle at the forefront of my mind. When I meet someone whose views or actions are different from my own, I remind myself to be curious rather than critical. After all, the very thing you might judge in someone else could be a reflection of your own struggles—or even worse, their strength in an area where you are weak. They may silently and simultaneously be judging you.

No one should ever be pointing a finger, because as the saying goes, when you point a finger at someone, three fingers point back at you. Before rushing to blame or criticize someone, take a moment to look in the mirror. Reflecting on ourselves can often stop us from judging another while providing the clarity we may need to extend grace to others. After all, there is only one Supreme Judge—let Him hold the gavel.

# PRINCIPLE #49
## Control Your Movement: Don't Confuse Movement with Progress

---

*"Time is the most valuable thing a man can spend."*
—Theophrastus

---

"Don't confuse movement with progress." This profound statement was popularized by one of my favorite thespians of all time, Denzel Washington. In one of his commencement speeches, he said, "Don't confuse movement with progress. My mom told me, 'You can run in place all the time and never get anywhere.' Continue to strive, continue to have goals, continue to progress." We've all witnessed a little hamster running as fast as he can on his wheel but not even making it two steps farther than when he started. Doing more doesn't necessarily mean achieving more.

Denzel's words are profound and resonate deeply because, subconsciously, I understood this but lacked the words to articulate it until hearing that speech. I never wanted to waste my motions. I never wanted to be confusing my movement for progress. It's a truth I've often witnessed in others. You can probably think of a couple busy people while you're reading this chapter, who are constantly on the move, juggling countless ideas and tasks, yet never reaching their goals or fulfilling their purpose. Their energy, though abundant, is lacking direction. No one wants to be that person.

Despite technological advances designed to make life easier, many people today feel busier than they did 100 years ago. The shift from industrial to knowledge-based work has led to a culture where being busy is often mistaken for productivity, even if it doesn't yield meaningful results.

Modern technology—such as smartphones and social media—has created an "always-on" environment, blurring the lines between work and personal life. This may not create constant physical movement, but it creates a constant movement in our brain giving us this feeling of constant busyness. We also have an overwhelming abundance of choices in the society in which we live today. Many people have FOMO (fear of missing out). This pushes people into filling their schedules, choosing movement without reflection, progress or true intent.

We all have one thing in common that puts us on the same playing field, no matter what our race or ethnicity. We all have 24 hours to spend each day, yet some people seem to get way more accomplished in a day than others. Why is that? It's because of their intentional movement.

Kyle Kowalski gives us seven hypotheses in *Sloww* as to why people are choosing movement, or being busy, over progress and introspection.

1. Busyness as a badge of honor and trendy status symbol—or the glorification of busy—to show our importance, value, or self-worth in our fast-paced society
2. Busyness as job security—an outward sign of productivity and company loyalty
3. Busyness as FOMO (Fear of Missing Out)—spending is shifting from buying things ("have it all") to experiences ("do it all"), packing our calendars (and social media feeds with the "highlight reel of life")
4. Busyness as a byproduct of the digital age—our 24/7 connected culture is blurring the line between life and work; promoting multitasking and never turning "off"

5. Busyness as a time filler—in the age of abundance of choice, we have infinite ways to fill time (online and off) instead of leaving idle moments as restorative white space
6. Busyness as necessity—working multiple jobs to make ends meet while also caring for children at home
7. Busyness as escapism—from idleness and slowing down to face the tough questions in life (e.g. Maybe past emotional pain or deep questions like, "What is the meaning of life?" or "What is my purpose?")

Stop for one moment. Take a deep breath and intentionally control your movement. Doesn't that feel good? Controlling your movement means being intentional with every action and not just filling your day with busyness. Each step you take should align with your purpose, fulfill your potential, and glorify the Most High. Progress isn't just about personal success; it's about inspiring others and uplifting those around you. When your actions are rooted in purpose, they create ripples that elevate your peers and community. Something that simply being busy cannot do.

Equally as important as controlling your movement is discernment—knowing when an opportunity aligns with your goals and when it may lead you astray. As noted in Kowalski's report, not all movement is good movement. Accepting opportunities just to stay busy can sometimes be a step backward or the first step toward your demise. Be very careful when choosing your steps and align them with your goals. As my grandmother used to say, "Baby, if you take one step, God will take two," but those steps must be strategic, grounded in faith, discernment, and wisdom.

There will be times when you may stumble or feel like you failed. You didn't fail—and it's not the end—you just learned a lesson. Pick yourself up and focus on your next step of progression. Turn missteps into learning opportunities. This principle is simple to understand but difficult to implement because it demands self-awareness, faith, and intentionality. It can be hard to know what's the right thing or what's the wrong thing. Stay rooted in who you are and what you want. This way you are not making decisions blindly. Life's treadmill can tempt us into motion for motion's sake, but true progress requires stepping off that treadmill and walking with intention, purpose and progression.

# PRINCIPLE #50
## The 50% Rule

---

*"When you wake up, your glass is already half full; it's up to you to fill up the remainder of the glass."* —Jock McKissic

---

Growing up, I always heard people talking about looking at the glass from a perspective of half full instead of half empty. As a child, I didn't fully understand it. I thought to myself, *what does that even mean*, but as I got older, it started making sense. I was in seventh grade when I made the basketball team. We were choosing numbers, and my first instinct was to choose 34 because Shaquille O'Neal was my idol. *Yeah, Shaq—34*, I said to myself. Then, I thought it would be better to pick a number that was personal and really meant something to me. I didn't pick a number that first day.

I went home and gave it some thought. The glass-half-full idea popped into my head. The glass is already 50% full—so I chose number 50. My young mind had grasped the concept that a half-full glass meant God had already given me things to help me be a great basketball player: my height, my coordination, my determination, even the discipline that was instilled in me at an early age—all were contributions to my glass. All I had to do was fill my glass 50% more to reach the top. Every time I put my jersey on it could serve as a reminder that it was up to me to fill it the rest of the way. I could fill it by working hard, being dedicated, and by giving my best effort on the court.

The day that I chose my number I randomly asked my grandmother when she was born, and when she told me 1935. I quickly did the math and realized that when I was born, she was 50 years old. That sealed it for me. I wore number 50 as a reminder of the glass being half full and how I could fill it the rest of the way. I chose the number 50 in the seventh grade, and it has stuck with me throughout my life, at every level.

Even after retiring from sports, I kept that number with me. My production company is called "Fifty Stories Entertainment." When people ask me why I love the number 50, I tell them it's because of the principle of looking at glass as half full and isn't just about sports—it's a life lesson. This number has become such a part of me that a lot of people call me 50 or J-50 instead of Jock.

In college sometimes interviewers asked me, "Why do you wear the number 50?"

I often replied with a little joke, "Where's the center of the football field?"

They'd say, "The 50-yard line."

"Yeah. I'm the center of attention, that's why I chose the number 50."

We'd laugh, and then I'd tell them the real story behind it.

The reason why I kept this number with me and even branded it into my company is because looking at the glass half-full is a way of reminding people to have a more positive perspective. It's about starting your day with gratitude, knowing that the glass is already half full, before your feet even hit the floor, and it's up to you to fill it up the rest of the way throughout the day.

When I first started acting, I knew it would be difficult to land the roles I wanted because I'm 6'7," and there weren't many people who looked like me in the industry at the time. Often, you'd see characters who looked like me in the background, just playing roles like a bodyguard, which is cool, but a lot of those roles don't have much depth or backstory. The viewers don't really know much about them. I wanted more than that; I wanted to be the one with a meaningful story.

The only actors I admired who were in similar positions were Michael Clarke Duncan and Forest Whitaker. So, when I began my acting career, I knew I had to prove myself. The acting industry is all about showing what you can do. Producers and casting directors don't really believe you until they see you in action, and then they might jump on the bandwagon.

I decided to take things into my own hands. I started writing short films and web series, creating characters that were different from the ones I would typically be cast as. I wrote my character as the traditional single dad or leading man/hot guy type—it worked. I started getting noticed, and eventually I landed an agent.

In the Bible, Philippians 4:13 says, "I can do all things through Christ who strengthens me." This verse ties directly to the 50% Rule. The strength to fill the rest of the glass is not solely ours; it is bolstered by the divine gifts we've already been given. These gifts—our talents, opportunities, and even our struggles—represent the "half full." Recognizing this allows us to see every challenge as a chance to *pour* more into our lives.

My ultimate goal was always to get into producing. I wanted to create my own opportunities, hire myself, and work with people I liked. That's always been part of the plan—I knew that one day I would have the chance to hire others I admire and build something from the ground up. That aligns perfectly with the "glass half full" mindset. It's not just about waiting for opportunities; it's about taking action and filling the glass yourself.

When we adopt the 50% Rule, we empower ourselves to meet life halfway. The glass isn't just a metaphor; it's a mirror reflecting our ability to co-create our reality. It's not about denying the challenge, but about acknowledging what's already there and using it as a foundation to move forward in the direction of your dreams. As Tony Robbins says, "Life is happening for us, not to us."

To truly unlock your potential, start by embracing the idea that your glass is already half full. By adopting this mindset, you can empower yourself to act, knowing that your path is already halfway paved with opportunity. When you see yourself as 50% full, it's easier to take ownership of your life. You embrace what has already been provided and take on the responsibility to fill the rest—not out of obligation, but out of the joy and fulfillment that comes from turning potential into reality.

As you close this book, remember: God has already filled your glass half full, and he's allowing you the pleasure of choosing the other half. The key to success is not in waiting for your circumstances to change, but in believing that the fullness of life is already within you. Tap into that fullness with every action, every effort, and every dream you pursue. By doing this, you'll not only witness your dreams taking form but also realize the power you have already been given—and that's when your life goes from—half full to overflowing!

# Conclusion

Life is a journey filled with twists, turns, and countless opportunities for growth. The 50 principles outlined in this book are more than just lessons—they are intended to help you thrive in every aspect of your life. When applied, they become tools to help you navigate challenges, seize opportunities, and unlock your full potential.

From embracing your foundation to leaning into your insecurities, and from building resilience to loving boldly, these principles remind us that thriving is not about perfection; it's about showing up, learning, and growing every single day. They call us to reflect on our experiences, embrace discomfort as a catalyst for change, and remain committed to our goals even when the path forward feels uncertain.

Applying these 50 principles in your life requires intention, effort, and patience. They challenge you to take accountability for your actions, practice self-awareness, and approach life with a mindset of continuous improvement. With each principle you integrate into your journey, you strengthen your foundation, expand your perspective, and deepen your sense of purpose.

These principles are not just about achieving success—they are about creating a life that resonates with your values, builds meaningful connections, and leaves a lasting impact. As you carry these lessons forward, apply them not only to your personal goals but also to your relationships, your passions, and the way you show up in the world.

Your journey is unique, and the possibilities ahead are limitless. By making a commitment to reading and applying these principles, you are equipping yourself with the tools to overcome obstacles, celebrate progress, and live authentically. Remember, every step you take is an opportunity to grow, inspire others, and thrive boldly.

You've got this. Now go out and thrive—one principle at a time.

Jock